Mona Hamadeh grew up in Lebanon. She spent her school holidays in the beautiful mountains where she was born, and where she developed a love of cooking from her grandmother, her mother and her aunts. Her passion for Lebanese food and cooking remained with her when she came to the UK as a young woman. She raised her own large family on a healthy Lebanese diet and now she passes it on to her grandchildren, who also recognise the importance of sharing and taking part in food preparation. This is Mona's third book where she shares again, not only her continuing passion for the delicious flavours that exemplify Lebanese food, but also the healthy properties of the superfoods that are a natural part of the diet that the Lebanese have enjoyed for generations.

Also by Mona Hamadeh

Everyday Lebanese Cooking
A Lebanese Feast of Vegetables, Pulses, Herbs and Spices

The Healthy Lebanese Family Cookbook

MONA HAMADEH

ROBINSON

First published in Great Britain in 2018
by Robinson

10 9 8 7 6 5 4 3 2 1

A CIP catalogue record for this book
is available from the British Library.

ISBN: 978-1-47213-871-2

Typeset in FF Quadraat
Designed by Andrew Barron @ Thextension
Printed and bound in Italy by L.E.G.O. S.p.A.

Papers used by Robinson are from
well-managed forests and other
responsible sources.

Robinson
An imprint of
Little, Brown Book Group
Carmelite House
50 Victoria Embankment
London EC4Y 0DZ

An Hachette UK Company
www.hachette.co.uk

www.littlebrown.co.uk

NOTES
All vegetables are medium unless
otherwise stated. Eggs are medium
unless otherwise stated. Herbs are
fresh unless otherwise stated.

Contents

Conversion charts

Weight

METRIC	IMPERIAL
25g	1oz
50g	2oz
75g	3oz
100g	4oz
150g	5oz
175g	6oz
200g	7oz
225g	8oz
250g	9oz
300g	10oz
350g	12oz
400g	14oz
450g	1lb

Oven temperatures

CELSIUS	FAHRENHEIT
110°C	225°F
120°C	250°F
140°C	275°F
150°C	300°F
160°C	325°F
180°C	350°F
190°C	375°F
200°C	400°F
220°C	425°F
230°C	450°F
240°C	475°F

Measurements

METRIC	IMPERIAL
5cm	2in
10cm	4in
13cm	5in
15cm	6in
18cm	7in
20cm	8in
25cm	10in
30cm	12in

Liquids

METRIC	IMPERIAL	US CUP
5ml	1 tsp	1 tsp
15ml	1 tbsp	1 tbsp
50ml	2fl oz	3 tbsp
60ml	2½fl oz	¼ cup
75ml	3fl oz	⅓ cup
100ml	4fl oz	scant ½ cup
125ml	4½ oz	½ cup
150ml	5fl oz	⅔ cup
200ml	7fl oz	scant 1 cup
250ml	9fl oz	1 cup
300ml	½ pint	1¼ cups
350ml	12fl oz	1⅓ cups
400ml	¾ pint	1¾ cups
500ml	17fl oz	2 cups
600ml	1 pt	2½ cups

Clockwise from above: roasted aubergines with pitta and garlic yogurt; my grandchildren making open pizza with spinach; the wonderful colours of fresh swiss chard.

1

Introduction to Healthy Lebanese Cooking

Opposite:
A fresh fruit seller at the roadside in the Chouf mountains.

Eating a Healthy, Balanced Diet

A healthy balanced diet should include the widest possible range of ingredients in order to deliver the full range of nutritional requirements. It should include:

Whole grains
Vegetables (a wide variety, including roots and leaves)
Fresh fruits
Nuts
Legumes (pulses and beans)
Herbs and spices
Protein sources
(meat, poultry, fish and dairy)
Oils, especially olive oil

Lebanese cuisine delivers everything listed above, easily, economically and with great flavours that all the family will enjoy.

Lebanese Food is a Superfood

People often ask me why the Lebanese diet is considered one of the healthiest in the world. For me, though, it's just the food we eat every day – it's what we were brought up on and we love all the flavours. I suppose the reason for its healthy reputation is the fact that so many foods used in Lebanese cooking are superfoods. And that's been the case long before anyone ever heard of the term.

Lebanese families have lived on this kind of food for centuries, and generation after generation has continued to bring its children up on this healthy diet, from the moment the babies were introduced to solid food. Consequently, Lebanese children grow up accustomed, not only to the delicious and varied flavours that their diet offers, but also to a natural, healthy, everyday eating routine. It is most unusual to see overweight children in the rural areas of Lebanon. It is a different matter, of course, where children have access to processed fast food.

In Lebanon, we're blessed with this delicious healthy food; it's our normal diet and even traditional street fast food is healthy and nutritious.

Superfoods are now very trendy and are what everyone is talking about. I began to look into it, researching and learning about the nutritional value of Lebanese food. And now I understand why the diet that I grew up on and have so enjoyed passing on to my own children, and to their children, is known as one of the healthiest in the world!

Learning to Cook Authentic Lebanese Food

My mother and her two sisters were great cooks, not adventurous but brilliant at what they knew. I loved cooking from a very young age and as a child, when in the village, it was fascinating to spend every opportunity I could hanging around these good cooks. I learnt so much from them. These times have stayed with me and were especially memorable when I could help. This is why I enjoy my grandchildren helping me in the kitchen. I hope I am helping to create for them the same memories and love of cooking.

These three sisters were so traditional and set in their own ways (they were a really funny bunch). My father worked abroad a lot of the time, so my mother took care of our own crop of olives every year. She loved eating out

Clockwise from above: Watermelons in season; shopping at a fish market; carob molasses – often used as a natural sweetener. It is also mixed with tahini for dipping bread into at breakfast.

Clockwise from left:
The Lebanese eat
a huge amount of
vegetables and fresh
fruit; sharing dishes at a
Beirut diner; an ancient
cedar of Lebanon in the
Chouf Mountains.

in restaurants, but never left the house without a small bottle of her own olive oil in her bag to drizzle on her food. She would rather use her own than use the restaurant's oil, believing her home pressed oil to be the best! Her sisters believed they were the best cooks, using only fresh, natural ingredients and were reluctant to eat outside their homes, especially aunt Souraya. She was a peasant who lived a primitive life in the mountains, not even having a sink in her kitchen, but having to wash her dishes outside where she had access to water. When it came to food, she ate only fresh, organic food.

Lebanese Food Culture

In spite of the unsettled political situation in the Middle East, the Lebanese continue to enjoy life to the full. They are a fun-loving nation and most hospitable. This is demonstrated by their approach to food. When visiting a Lebanese, you should expect to have food offered even if your visit is unexpected. Refusal to eat is unacceptable and will offend your host. Food is the main focus and is all about sharing – it is never plated but is placed in the middle of the table for everyone to share. All meals are prolonged and considered social occasions and are never to be rushed – they are times for the family to gather round the table and enjoy the food while catching up. Your Lebanese host will keep asking you to eat more because we are mortified at the thought of our guest not having enough food. The Lebanese say: it's all about sharing bread and salt, which means love and friendship. We even love talking about food while eating it!

The majority of people in the rural areas of Lebanon live to a very old age. Disabling arthritis, colon cancer, diabetes and high cholesterol are rare. These common diseases in western countries are attributed to refined and processed food, too much meat, sugar and dairy. Interestingly, studies suggest that colon cancer has decreased in the last five years, which is due to more people eating healthier fresh Mediterranean food.

What the Lebanese Eat

Apart from being healthy, Lebanese food is quite low in calories but you never have to leave the table hungry. It is both satisfying and enjoyable. The Lebanese eat a huge amount of vegetables and fresh fruit. The majority of the dishes include vegetables or pulses. Meat is not used in big quantities and is consumed, on average, only once a week. On the whole, the Lebanese love meat-free days. Often, country people go foraging for seasonal vegetables such as wild asparagus, leeks, spinach and wild fennel. You don't find many vegetarians in Lebanon, but many of the dishes are vegetarian and vegan anyway.

Fish is part of our basic diet and is plentiful and affordable. All fish are caught locally, with fishermen catching seasonal fish and selling it on the same day. Even in rural areas that are far from the sea, people are able to buy fish from fish sellers who come to the village most days.

Fish provides high-quality protein, vitamins and minerals and is low in calories. All types of fish are very popular, especially whitebait, which are available only during the summer season and are bought by the kilo, fried and served a little crispy – these are a real favourite. There are many fish recipes and some specialities in certain areas.

The Lebanese never eat desserts after a meal, preferring to serve fresh fruit instead because it's so refreshing after a filling meal. Sweets and cakes are eaten, but at other times, as treats.

In cities, there are countless high-quality patisseries and bakeries in every street. The Lebanese often stop at these to collect sweets as a gift when visiting someone, as is the custom. We never deny ourselves the occasional unhealthy treat, knowing that treating ourselves in this way doesn't happen often.

Water is the number-one favourite drink. A jug of water is always present on the table, and you even get a glass of water with every cup of coffee. Some people still prefer to get their water directly from the springs running down the mountains. Coffee is the most common hot drink, served black in a small cup, and is similar to Turkish coffee. Tea is drunk occasionally; we tend to prefer drinks made with cinnamon, aniseed or ginger, or all combined together.

It's better to buy organic food when possible, but sometimes it's unavailable and for many people it's unaffordable. More important are fresh, natural ingredients and the avoidance of processed food. We use only extra virgin olive oil for cooking which stems from living in the mountains where there is an abundance of olive oil. In fact, many people still use it even for frying chips, fish and vegetables. In the past, the older generation didn't even know other types of oil existed! Now the nutritional and health-enhancing properties of olive oil are well known.

In Lebanon, we are blessed with having fresh fruit and vegetables all year round. This is because we have 300 days of sunshine a year, rich soil, a great climate and plenty of water. All fruit, and therefore fresh fruit juices, are a good source of vitamin C.

About this Book

The recipes in this book are suitable for all the family. In the UK, I always serve Lebanese food whenever I have guests, and it's always enjoyed by adults and children alike, even by people who have previously claimed they didn't like foreign food!

Many people who bought my previous books said how surprised they were that Lebanese food is so simple to prepare. The magic of Lebanese food is that most recipes have only a few ingredients and yet you can turn them into a tasty dish. And the variety is endless, so we never tire of eating it.

The recipes here are tasty, highly nutritious, filling and affordable and most ingredients used are available in western supermarkets and food stores. Recipes are mostly authentic, but some have a modern approach and include ingredients introduced to the Lebanese in recent years. The recipes are sugar-free, low-fat, low-cholesterol, low-calorie and mostly gluten-free. It is not the norm to use dairy in cooking (apart from the exception of a few yogurt dishes).

The Lebanese way is always to serve plenty of food, with no portion control, but with this kind of food, you don't need to worry about how much you eat, because most recipes are exceptionally low in calories. Eating Lebanese cuisine is one way of living healthily, and is a natural way to control your weight without going hungry.

BREAD

Bread is the main source of carbohydrate in Lebanon. To the majority of people it is essential, but with the gluten-free trend these days, many people have given up bread and all food made with flour. Many researchers believe it's unnecessary unless you suffer from coeliac disease. The Lebanese, however, love their bread and it's always present with breakfast, lunch and dinner. When eating we usually pick up food and dips with a piece of (flat) bread.

RAW VEGETABLES

A large plate with a selection of raw vegetables is often placed on the table. The vegetables are for dipping and are also used to accompany many dishes. We just love munching on raw vegetables, such as lettuces, cucumbers, radishes, peppers, chilli, carrots and even fresh mint leaves. Uncooked vegetables maintain all their vitamins, especially vitamin C.

THE MOUNEH

It is traditional for every Lebanese home to create a store (*mouneh*) from summer and autumn produce to provide food during the winter. These stores include pickles, zaatar, sumac, olives, labneh in olive oil, bulgur wheat and much more.

2

Main Common Ingredients

Opposite:
Time to pick some
olives!

Top: A family picking their olives; left and above: at the local olive press and store room.

In Lebanon, for centuries people have owned land on which they mainly grow olive trees. In my village there are many ancient olive trees, including some pre-Roman. And new olive trees are always being planted in more commercial areas. Landowners start harvesting their olives in November and December, and then take them to the local olive press where they hang around for hours while the olives are being pressed. It is the annual ritual that people look forward to. Walking around the village, during this special time always takes me back to my childhood, seeing people harvesting their olives, with the aroma of the olives in the air. The fresh oil, which looks cloudy and is aromatic with a very strong flavour, is taken home and eaten with a traditional dish of fresh flatbread. Known as beaye, each olive-oil soaked piece of bread is spread with roasted onions and pomegranate seeds and rolled into a wrap (only a very strong stomach can manage this).

People take huge pride in their harvest and compete over whose oil tastes the best. As I mentioned earlier, the Lebanese don't eat much meat. We use plenty of olive oil, which as well as adding flavour to dishes also makes food substantial and satisfying. A jug of olive oil is always present on the table. Olive oil is also used for preserving pickled vegetables and cheeses, which can be stored in a cool, dark environment to maintain the flavour for up to a year. Surplus oil is cooked and turned into pure soap, which is made at home.

OLIVE OIL

Olive oil is a basic ingredient in the Mediterranean diet and this is a key reason as to why this diet is claimed to be the healthiest.

All Lebanese oil is virgin olive oil. More and more people have switched to using virgin olive oil. It adds flavour, especially when used on salads, in dips and on any finished cooked food. You can't beat dipping fresh crusty bread in good-quality olive oil.

Olive oil is rich in monounsaturated fats that reduce the risk of heart diseases and type-2 diabetes. It also reduces cholesterol and high-blood pressure. Studies have shown that the unsaturated fats found in olive oil, seeds and nut oil are more effective in reducing the incidence of these diseases than a low-fat diet, by up to 50 per cent. It also protects blood vessels by triggering changes to the system of defence against oxidants, as well as helping the walls of these vessels to remain strong.

OLIVES

Olives are very popular in Lebanon. A bowl of olives is always present with breakfast, lunch and dinner. Normally, we finish a meal with a few olives and bread. This indicates that you have finished eating and are ending the meal. When I have guests for dinner in Lebanon, if ever it slips my mind to put olives on the table, my guests ask for them to complete the meal.

TAHINI

Tahini is a paste made from roasted sesame seeds. It is high in fat, therefore high in calories and contains monounsaturated and polyunsaturated fat, which are good fats. Tahini is known to lower cholesterol and helps to ease the symptoms of other diseases, such as osteoarthritis. In Lebanese cuisine, tahini is used very often as a salad dressing, in dips and sauces and sometimes in cooking. Tahini makes delicious food and is sold in most supermarkets and specialised shops and can be stored in your kitchen cupboard for many months.

Bulgur Wheat (Burghul)

Bulgur wheat, or burghul, is a whole grain. It is frequently used in Lebanese cuisine and villagers buy the wheat, boil it to cook it well, then spread it on sheets in the sun for several days to dry before it's taken to the local mill to be crushed. It is then stored for use during the year as part of the *mouneh*, which means food to store. It is also commercially sold everywhere. If you can get it, the wholewheat bulgur wheat is best. Bulgur wheat is high in fibre, which regulates sugar levels in the blood, blocks the absorption of cholesterol and is filling, which helps when trying to lose weight. It also contains iron and protein. When the wheat is milled it can be produced in different sized grains and then selected, as required, in the dish.

Rice

Apart from bread, rice is the main source of carbohydrate in the Lebanese diet and is consumed most days in one way or another. Brown rice contains fibre and therefore is the healthier option. Rice is a cereal grain and is the most widely consumed staple food for more than half the world's population.

Freekeh

Freekeh is an ancient super grain that's been a staple in the Middle Eastern diet for centuries. It is picked while the wheat is still young and green, then the soft grains are roasted then broken. It is slightly chewy, but is delicious and is loaded with nutritional

benefits. It is low in fat and high in protein and fibre. Freekeh has now become a new trend in western countries as a superfood because it contains a higher amount of protein than quinoa and a very high percentage of fibre.

Tomatoes

Tomatoes contain a very high level of antioxidants, especially lycopene, and have more health benefits than most popular fruits. Lycopene is important for bones, especially in menopausal women. Tomatoes are also rich in vitamin C and in potassium, the latter of which helps to regulate the heart rate and controls blood pressure. Tomatoes are a big part of the Lebanese diet and are used in salads and as the main ingredient for sauces in cooking.

Lemons

We use lemons in large quantities in cooking and salads and to squeeze over our food. They are highly nutritious and an excellent source of vitamin C. They contain 8 per cent citric acid, which is a natural preservative and helps digestion. They also contain minerals, such as iron, potassium, calcium and copper. Potassium is an important component that regulates the heart rate and controls blood pressure.

Clockwise from above:
pulses (legumes);
dried and ground
sumac flowers; zaatar.

3

Typical Lebanese Breakfasts

Opposite:
Mint leaves, olives,
cucumber and
tomatoes, eggs
with tomatoes, *foul
mdammas, labneh,
za'atar*, olive oil, white
cheeses and dried fruit.

In Lebanon, we can choose from a big variety of very different breakfast foods. Here are the main choices:

Cheeses are mostly eaten at breakfast. Labneh, zaatar with olive oil, olives, tomatoes, cucumber and fresh mint leaves add a great taste of freshness. When time permits, other dishes are served, such as *foul mdammas* (dried broad beans with lemon dressing), eggs cooked in various ways and *manoushis* (very thin pizzas topped with thyme and olive oil or grated halloumi cheese or minced lamb and tomatoes). *Manoushi* bakeries are available everywhere – they are classed as fast street food to eat on the go and the food is very economical.

Breakfast cafés are popular and are busy from early morning to midday. You find them everywhere in cities, towns and villages, serving *foul mdammas*, hummus, various egg dishes and *fetteh* (chickpeas and toasted pitta topped with garlic yogurt).

Some say breakfast is the most important meal of the day and some disagree. Personally, it's the meal I enjoy the most and I always made sure my children had breakfast before leaving the house. I love mornings and the start of the day, and enjoying breakfast with a cup of coffee forces you to start gently, calmly, and to refuel yourself, whether you had a good night's sleep or a restless night.

The sweet option is *knafeh*, a white cheese base topped with buttery semolina, baked to brown. This is served with syrup and a ring of bread coated with sesame seeds. *Knafeh* is sold at patisseries from early to late morning. This is the less healthy option but it is delicious enough to indulge in occasionally.

Eggs with Lamb
Bayd B Kawarma

Traditional *kawarma* is made with lamb fat and meat and salt. It's used for cooking with, which removes the need for any oil or meat in the dish and it can be stored for months. It is popularly used for frying eggs. For this recipe, I cook the eggs with minced lamb as they do in restaurants these days and it is equally as delicious with less fat than the traditional *kawarma*.

SERVES **2**

PREPARATION TIME
none

COOKING TIME
10 minutes

200g minced lamb
4 free-range eggs
A sprinkle of black pepper (optional)
A sprinkle of ground cinnamon (optional)
Salt

1 In a frying pan, fry the minced lamb over a medium heat for 5 minutes and stir until it becomes slightly brown and crispy.

2 Crack the eggs over the meat and allow the egg whites to cook and set. The egg yolks should be soft unless you prefer them well cooked. Some people prefer the yolks burst and combined with the white.

3 Season with salt and sprinkle with pepper or cinnamon or both and serve with bread.

Concentrated Yogurt Spread
Labneh

Labneh is always popular at breakfast either as a dip or used as a spread on bread in order to make a wrap. Sometimes it's served with starters (*maza*), mixed with crushed garlic, olives and fresh mint leaves. There is always *labneh* in every Lebanese fridge.

SERVES 6 OR MORE

PREPARATION TIME
5 minutes, plus draining time

COOKING TIME
none

COOK'S TIP
A large quantity of *labneh* can be rolled into a small ball, stored in a jar and covered with olive oil. The jar should be kept in a cool place or in the fridge and will keep for several months.

1 tsp salt
2 litres natural yogurt (see page 236)
Olive oil, to taste
Mint leaves to serve

1 Stir the salt into the yogurt and pour the mixture into a muslin bag. Place the bag over a colander over the sink or hang it on a tap. If using a muslin cloth, spread the cloth on a colander placed in a bowl and pour the yogurt onto it.

2 Allow the yogurt to drain overnight. Remove the yogurt from the bag or cloth, spread it on a plate and drizzle it with olive oil.

3 Serve with bread for dipping, olives, tomatoes, cucumber and mint leaves. Mint goes beautifully with *labneh*. *Labneh* keeps in the fridge for up to a week.

Eggs with Chilli Tomatoes
Bayd Ma Banadoura

When I am in my village, I often get invited for breakfast and this is one of the dishes served. It also makes a quick and filling but light meal.

SERVES 4

PREPARATION TIME
5 minutes

COOKING TIME
15–20 minutes

1 Sauté the onion with the olive oil in a frying pan over a medium heat, for 10 minutes until golden. Add the garlic and fry for another minute. Stir in the chilli or cayenne pepper, if using.

2 Add the chopped tomatoes, stir and cook for 5 minutes. Season with salt.

3 Crack the eggs over the tomatoes and stir gently, so the eggs are combined with the tomatoes and onion. Cook for a few minutes until the eggs are cooked through.

4 Sprinkle with cinnamon and black pepper and serve with bread and some mint leaves.

1 onion (about 100g), finely chopped
30ml olive oil
2 garlic cloves, sliced
1 red chilli, chopped, or ½ tsp cayenne pepper
  (optional)
400g ripe tomatoes, chopped
5 free-range eggs
½ tsp ground cinnamon
Pinch of black pepper
Mint leaves, to serve
Salt

Dried Broad Beans with Lemon Dressing
Foul Mdammas

This superb dish bursts with both flavour and goodness and is loved by every Lebanese. It is always served with fresh vegetables such as tomatoes, mint leaves, chilli and radishes, on the side, and with bread. There are even speciality cafés that serve only this dish and open only until late morning. However, it is easy enough to make at home. Buy the beans dried or tinned.

SERVES 4

PREPARATION TIME
10 minutes, plus soaking if using dried beans

COOKING TIME
1 hour, if using dried beans

250g dried or 500g cooked tinned broad beans, drained, water reserved
2 garlic cloves, crushed
1 tsp salt
juice of 1 lemon (about 30ml)
30ml olive oil
2 tomatoes (about 200g), chopped
5g parsley, chopped

1 If using dried beans, soak them overnight. Drain and boil them in water for about 1 hour until the beans are very tender and soft.

2 Drain the beans, reserving a little of the water to use as stock. Put the drained beans or beans from a tin in a bowl and smash them slightly with a fork.

3 Make a dressing by mixing the garlic, salt and lemon juice together. Pour the dressing over the beans and stir to combine. If the beans look too dry, add a little of the stock. If you used tinned broad beans, used a little water.

4 Finally, top each portion with chopped tomatoes and parsley and drizzle with the olive oil.

Wild Thyme and Olive Oil Dip with Pitta Breads
Zaatar Wzeit

The first time my British husband visited Lebanon he was quite surprised to see my very young nephews and nieces having their breakfast sitting on the floor around a tray with bread, zaatar and olive oil on it. The children were chatting and giggling while tearing off pieces of bread to dip in the zaatar and oil. Now dipping bread in oil has become a trend in the West.

SERVES 4

PREPARATION TIME
5 minutes

COOKING TIME
2–4 minutes

COOK'S TIP
Slightly warm the bread so it's easier to split. You can also use this mixture as a dip and tear the bread for dipping into the oil and zaatar.

4–6 pitta breads
35g zaatar, mixed with 8g sumac and
    15g sesame seeds, slightly toasted
60ml olive oil

1 Heat a frying pan then dry fry the sesame seed and keep turning them for 1–2 minutes until they begin to brown very slightly.

2 Open up the bread. Mix the zaatar mixture with the oil to make a paste and spread it on the inside of the bread before putting the bread back together.

3 Grill each side of the sandwiched *zaatar wzeit* for 1–2 minutes, until both sides are toasted and a little crispy.

4 Serve with tomatoes, mint and cucumber.

Curd and Honey with Bread
Kashta Wasal

Curd and honey goes back centuries. It resembles ricotta cheese and is served after a meal or at breakfast. Once, after having breakfast in a café with a friend up in the mountains, we noticed *kashta* and honey being served with hot fresh bread – though we were full, we ordered a plate because it is just too delicious to resist!

SERVES 4–6

PREPARATION TIME
1–2 minutes

COOKING TIME
20 minutes

COOK'S TIP
Kashta is sometimes served with sliced bananas or strawberries.

200g honey
20g pistachios, chopped
20g pine nuts (optional)

1 Simply spread the *kashta* on a serving plate. To make the *kashta*, see page 243.

2 Drizzle the honey all over the top and sprinkle it with the nuts.

3 Serve with warm fresh bread or on its own if served as a dessert.

4

A Selection of Maza Dishes for Sharing

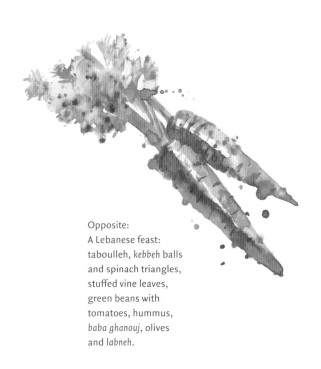

Opposite:
A Lebanese feast:
taboulleh, *kebbeh* balls
and spinach triangles,
stuffed vine leaves,
green beans with
tomatoes, hummus,
baba ghanouj, olives
and *labneh*.

Maza is a selection of small portions of various dishes and is usually served with an assortment of vegetable dishes. We always include a large plate of raw vegetables to pick at or to use for dipping as an alternative to bread. It is the favourite way to spend a few hours with friends and family chatting, dipping your bread in the food and sharing all your favourite dishes placed in the middle of the table for everyone to share.

Tabbouleh is the national dish and is served with the maza in restaurants or at home. A meal is never complete without it. Even at home it is always served with other starters or as the starter.

The Lebanese take great pleasure in eating and enjoying food and the maza is certainly the best part of a Lebanese meal. We often go out and enjoy it and forget about ordering a main course. In this chapter, I have selected the basic starters.

Arak is the national drink usually served with this kind of food. It is slightly sweet and compatible with the lemony food. It's made with grape juice and aniseed, has a high percentage of alcohol and is usually mixed with water.

Squid Provençale
Sbaidej Mtabal

Squid is always served with seafood starters, either dipped in breadcrumbs and fried, sometimes grilled, or served with lemon and garlic sauce – we call this squid Provençale. French is commonly spoken in Lebanon.

SERVES 4

PREPARATION TIME
15 minutes

COOKING TIME
3 minutes

COOK'S TIP
Take care when cooking the squid – overcooking it makes it tough and very chewy.

1 Heat the oil in a frying pan over a low heat and stir in the garlic, cooling for a few seconds. Do not allow the garlic to brown.

2 Add the coriander and stir for a few more seconds.

3 Add the squid and fry for 1 minute, then add the lemon juice and cook for another 1 minute. Remove from the heat.

4 Season with salt and serve at once with bread.

30ml olive oil
2 garlic cloves, chopped
25g coriander, chopped
300g squid, chopped or sliced
Juice of 1 lemon (about 30ml)
Salt

Traditional Lebanese Herb and Bulgur Wheat Salad
Tabbouleh

Tabbouleh is the most traditional salad in Lebanon. I should say dish because apart from being packed with nutrients, tabbouleh is served as a starter and as part of the maza. You never see a spread for an occasion or eating opportunity without it.

SERVES 4

PREPARATION TIME
30 minutes

COOKING TIME
None

COOK'S TIP
You may prepare tabbouleh in advance and keep it in the fridge. Stir in the dressing, salt and *burghul* immediately before serving.

200g flat-leaf parsley, finely chopped
30g mint leaves, finely chopped
70g spring onions with leaves or 1 small onion, chopped
¼ tsp ground black pepper
500g tomatoes, chopped
60ml olive oil
Juice of 2–3 lemons (about 50ml)
25g fine bulgur wheat (burghul)
1 tsp salt

1 Rinse the parsley and mint with water and drain in a colander while preparing the remaining ingredients.

2 Put the onion in a bowl and rub with black pepper. This is to prevent the onions from smelling strong if they are not served soon. Add the tomatoes, oil and lemon juice and mix well together, then stir in the drained parsley and mint.

3 Add the bulgur wheat and salt just before serving so it has a little crunch.

4 The salad can also be served with lettuce leaves or sweet tender cabbage leaves.

Opposite:
Yasmina and Alex, the tabbouleh kids

Smoky Aubergine and Tahini Dip
Baba Ghanoug

This is one of the dishes that I have to include in every book as it is one of the most delicious and classic foods. It's one that has become internationally known.

SERVES 4

PREPARATION TIME
15 minutes

COOKING TIME
20 minutes

COOK'S TIP
You can freeze the cooked and peeled aubergines and use them as needed. Add the other ingredients before serving.

2 large aubergines (about 800g)
50ml tahini
2–3 garlic cloves, crushed
1 tsp salt
Juice of 1–2 lemons (about 30ml)

FOR THE GARNISH (ALL OPTIONAL)
Pomegranate seeds
Spring onions, chopped
Parsley or mint, chopped
Olive oil, to drizzle

1 Place the aubergines on the flame of a gas burner on the hob, turning them occasionally and making sure both ends are soft and well cooked. Once done, the skin will look really burnt. Leave them aside to cool. If you prefer not to have the smoky taste, prick the aubergines all over as they can sometimes explode, and roast them in a preheated oven at 220°C/Fan 200°C/Gas 7, for 20 minutes.

2 When the aubergines are cool enough to handle, peel the skin off and rinse the flesh under cold water to remove any black bits. Remove the top end with the stem and mash the flesh in a bowl using a fork or potato masher. (Avoid using a food processor to maintain the texture.)

3 Add the remaining ingredients and combine well.

4 Turn out onto a serving dish and garnish with my suggestions or just 1 of them and drizzle with olive oil, if using.

5 Serve with pitta bread for dipping. Keep in the fridge for up to a week.

Fish with Chard

Shawarma Samacke

It was just recently that I was served this dish, which was unique and tasty, as part of the maza selection. Chard is one of the most popular greens in Lebanon, especially the stalks.

200g green or rainbow chard stalks,
   cut into 3cm pieces
10ml olive oil
Pinch of salt, plus extra to season
150g chunky white fish fillet, cut into 4 pieces
10g plain flour
A little chopped parsley, to garnish

FOR THE TAHINI SAUCE
30ml tahini
1 garlic clove, crushed
Juice of ½–1 lemon (about 20ml)
Pinch of salt

1 Cook the chard stalks in salted, boiling water for 4 minutes. Turn out into a colander and leave it aside to drain well.

2 Meanwhile, prepare the tahini sauce by mixing all the sauce ingredients together in a bowl, until the mixture becomes thick. Thin it down with a little water so that it becomes creamy.

3 Heat the oil in a shallow pan, sprinkle a little salt on the fish, lightly coat with flour and fry each side over a medium heat for 2–3 minutes until lightly browned.

4 Place the chard on a serving plate, and drizzle the tahini sauce over the top, arrange the fish over the chard and garnish with chopped parsley.

5 Serve with lemon wedges and bread.

Feta Cheese with Chilli and Zaatar
Shankleesh

Shankleesh is a simple mixture but it's powerful in flavour. It's usually bought from dairy shops or the cheese counter in supermarkets. Because of its strong flavour, it is always served in small quantities with other ingredients mixed with it that make it into a delicious dip.

SERVES 4

PREPARATION TIME
5 minutes

COOKING TIME
none

200g feta cheese, crumbled
1 small onion (about 50g), finely chopped
1 hot red chilli, finely chopped
2 tsp zaatar (wild thyme), plus a little extra
  for sprinkling
100g tomatoes, chopped
1 tbsp olive oil

1 Mix the crumbled cheese with the onion, chilli and zaatar, making sure it stays fairly crumbly.

2 Place the shankleesh onto a serving plate and spread the chopped tomatoes over the top.

3 Drizzle with olive oil, sprinkle with a couple pinches of zaatar, and serve with bread or toasted pitta.

Red Chilli Potatoes
Batata Harrah

This tasty dish is usually served with starters (maza) as a flavoursome dish. In Lebanon, potatoes are not eaten as a source of carbohydrate but used only as an ingredient. I'm not a potato fan, but I enjoy this dish whenever it's served.

SERVES 4

PREPARATION TIME
15 minutes, plus draining

COOKING TIME
20 minutes

COOK'S TIP
If you want to avoid frying, roast the potatoes in the oven, then mix with the garlic, chilli and coriander and then roast for another 5 minutes.

500g potatoes, peeled and cubed
1 tsp chilli powder
1 tsp salt
40ml olive oil
4 garlic cloves, chopped
1 red chilli, deseeded and sliced
40g coriander, chopped, reserving a little to garnish

1 Rub the potato cubes with the chilli powder and salt. Then heat the oil in a frying pan over a medium heat and fry the potatoes for 15 minutes until they become a golden-red colour and appear crispy on the outside. Remove the potatoes using a slotted spoon and set aside to drain on kitchen paper.

2 Add the chopped garlic and sliced chilli to the pan and fry for a few seconds. Avoid letting the garlic brown.

3 Return the potatoes to the pan and turn over to combine with the garlic and chilli for a few seconds.

4 Stir in the coriander and cook for another 2 minutes. Remove the pan from the heat.

5 Serve hot, garnished with a little chopped coriander, with starters or as a side dish.

Hummus with Kafta Balls
Hummus B Kafta

Many people in the West are now familiar with hummus. It's always present as one of the maza dishes. It's often served with lamb, herbs and nuts. Kafta and hummus are a brilliant combination of flavours.

SERVES 4–6

PREPARATION TIME
20 minutes, plus soaking for the chickpeas, if dried

COOKING TIME
5 minutes, plus 1 hour, if using dried chickpeas

250g cooked or 125g dried chickpeas
100g tahini
3 garlic cloves, crushed
1 tsp salt
Juice of 1–2 lemons (about 50ml)
1 tomato, chopped, to garnish
10g parsley, chopped, to garnish

FOR THE KAFTA
200g minced lamb
15g parsley, finely chopped
1 small onion (about 40g), grated or finely chopped
¼ tsp ground cinnamon
¼ tsp ground black pepper
¼ tsp salt

1 If using dried chickpeas, soak them overnight. Drain and cook them with fresh water for about 1 hour. Make sure the chickpeas are well cooked and very soft in the centre, almost mushy.

2 While the chickpeas are cooking, prepare the kafta by mixing all the kafta ingredients together. Then roll the mixture with your hands into bite-sized balls.

3 Mash the cooked chickpeas by hand or in a food processor until they form a very smooth paste.

4 Add the tahini, garlic, salt and lemon juice to the chickpeas and mix well. The texture will look stiff and dry, so gradually add a little cold water while mixing until you have a creamy, smooth consistency. Place the hummus onto a serving plate.

5 Grill or griddle the kafta balls for 5 minutes until they are slightly brown and place them on top of the hummus.

6 Garnish with tomatoes and chopped parsley.

Pitta Crouton Salad
Fattoush

During the month of Ramadan, *fattoush* is always served at the beginning of the meal because it's light and refreshing. This salad is a popular alternative to the traditional tabbouleh (see page 30).

SERVES 4

PREPARATION TIME
20 minutes

COOKING TIME
None

COOK'S TIP
It's up to you whether you prefer to use lemon juice or vinegar. Some people prefer this dish with pomegranate molasses or balsamic vinegar for a modern option.

25g mint leaves, chopped
40g flat-leaf parsley, chopped
50g whole purslane leaves (optional and subject to availability)
400g tomatoes, chopped
200g cucumber, chopped
80g spring onions with leaves, trimmed and chopped
6 radishes, trimmed and sliced
1 green or red pepper (about 120g), deseeded and chopped
140g cos or iceberg lettuce leaves, thinly sliced
2–3 pitta bread (about 150g), toasted
50–70g pomegranate seeds (optional)

FOR THE DRESSING
2 garlic cloves, crushed
½ tsp salt
½ tbsp sumac
Juice of 1 lemon (about 30ml) or 30ml red or white wine vinegar
50ml olive oil

1 Place all the prepared herbs and vegetables in a bowl.

2 To make the dressing, place the garlic, salt, sumac, lemon juice or vinegar, and olive oil in a bowl and combine, then pour over the salad and mix well.

3 Break the toasted pitta into small pieces and add the pieces to the salad just before serving.

4 Scatter the pomegranate seeds over the top, if using.

Little Fish Pies
Sambousac Samack

Sambousac is always served with the maza or with buffets. It is most commonly filled with minced meat and onions and fried. As many people are cutting down on red meat, the fish version is becoming increasingly popular.

MAKES 12

PREPARATION TIME
30 minutes

COOKING TIME
35 minutes

FOR THE PASTRY
200g plain flour, plus extra for rolling
50ml olive oil
¼ tsp salt

FOR THE FILLING
30ml olive oil, plus extra for brushing
2 onions (about 250g), halved and sliced
330g white fish fillet, cut into small cubes
½ tsp salt
½ tsp ground white pepper
10g parsley, chopped
1 lemon, cut into wedges, to serve

1 To prepare the pastry, rub the flour with the oil and the salt. Gradually add 100ml water to form a dough. Wrap the dough in cling film and keep it in the fridge while you prepare the filling.

2 Preheat the oven to 200°C/fan 180°C/gas 6. Heat the oil over a medium heat and sauté the onions for 10 minutes to brown slightly. Add the fish, salt and pepper, stir a little and cook for another 5 minutes. Now stir in the parsley.

3 Roll out the pastry thinly on a floured surface and cut out circles of 10cm in diameter.

4 Place 1 tablespoon of the filling on 1 half of the circle, fold over the other half and firmly press the edges together to seal well. Pinch 1 corner and twist, then work your way along the edge until you get to the other corner. Repeat steps 3 and 4 until you have used all the dough and filling.

5 Place the *sambousacs* on a baking tray lined with greaseproof paper, brush each one with oil and bake in the oven for 20 minutes until the *sambousacs* are brown.

6 Serve warm with lemon wedges on the side.

Smoky Aubergine Salad
Raheb

This very tasty salad is normally served as a starter or part of the maza. The smoked aubergine, herbs, lemon and garlic form such a fantastic combination of flavours. *Raheb* is light and very low in calories.

SERVES 4

PREPARATION TIME
20 minutes

COOKING TIME
15 minutes

2 large aubergines (about 500g)
25g spring onions, including leaves, trimmed
  and chopped
100g tomatoes, chopped
1 small–medium yellow or orange pepper
  (about 75g), diced
20g parsley leaves, chopped
5g mint leaves, chopped
Juice of 1 lemon (about 30ml)
2 garlic cloves, crushed
1 tsp salt
50g pomegranate seeds
20ml olive oil, for drizzling (optional)

1 Place the aubergines on the flame of a gas burner on the hob, turning them occasionally. Cook for 15 minutes until the skin looks burnt. Leave them aside to cool. The flesh of the aubergines should be soft.

2 While the aubergines are cooling, mix together the remaining vegetables and herbs with the lemon juice, crushed garlic, and salt.

3 Peel the skin off the aubergines and rinse the flesh under cold water to remove any bits of skin. Remove the top end with the stem, chop up the flesh and add it to the salad mixture.

4 Turn the salad out onto a serving dish and scatter the pomegranate seeds over the top.

5 Serve as a starter, with olive oil on the side to drizzle over the top if desired, and bread.

Red Split Lentils with Bulgur Wheat
Kebbeh Adas

I was told about this dish several times but it didn't appeal to me. In the end I decided to go for it and try it. I was amazed – it's not only healthy, but delicious too. Serve it as part of the maza spread or as a starter by itself with toasted flatbread on the side.

SERVES 4

PREPARATION TIME
15 minutes

COOKING TIME
30 minutes

COOK'S TIP
Semi-sweet pomegranates have dark red skin and deep red seeds. The sweet pomegranates have the paler, creamy colour and the seeds are pale pink. These are more suitable for desserts.

FOR THE KEBBEH
1 onion (about 135g), finely chopped
20ml olive oil
100g split orange lentils
250ml warm water
1 red pepper (about 100g)
1 green chilli, deseeded and chopped
¼ tsp chilli powder
1 tsp ground cumin
1 tsp salt
80g fine bulgur wheat (burghul)

FOR THE SALSA
130g tomatoes, chopped
1 green chilli, deseeded and sliced
40g semi-sweet pomegranate seeds (optional)
25g spring onions, chopped
1 garlic clove, crushed
1 tbsp lemon juice
10g mint leaves, chopped
20ml olive oil
Salt, to taste

1 Put the onion and oil in a pan and sauté the onion over a medium heat for about 5 minutes or until the onion is very soft and slightly golden.

2 Rinse the lentils and add them to the onion with 250ml of warm water. Cover and simmer over a low heat for about 20 minutes. Check the moisture: the lentils should be fluffy but not too dry and most of the moisture should be absorbed. Allow the lentils to cool.

3 After removing the stalk and seeds, blend the red pepper in a food processor and add it to the cooled lentils with the remaining kebbeh ingredients. Mix well and leave aside while you prepare the salsa. (If the mixture is too stiff, just add a little water.)

4 Mix all the salsa ingredients together and season with salt. Spread the lentil *kebbeh* on a flat serving plate and top with the salsa.

Hummus with Parsley and Pine Nuts
Hummus Beiruty

Most Beiruties would never serve hummus without parsley and pine nuts. Just a little extra effort adds a lot of flavour.

SERVES 4

PREPARATION TIME
20 minutes, plus soaking if using dried chickpeas

COOKING TIME
1 hour to cook the dried chickpeas, if using

250g cooked or 125g dried chickpeas
100g tahini
3 garlic cloves, crushed
1 tsp salt
Juice of 1–2 lemons (about 50ml)
20g parsley, chopped

FOR THE GARNISH
Reserved parsley
25g pine nuts
20ml olive oil (optional)

1 If using dried chickpeas, see page 39.

2 Mash the chickpeas by hand or with a food processor until you have a lump-free paste.

3 Add the tahini, garlic, salt and lemon juice and mix well. The texture will look stiff and dry, so gradually add a little cold water while mixing until you have a smooth, creamy consistency.

4 Mix in the parsley, reserving a little to garnish, and spread the hummus onto a serving plate.

5 Toast the pine nuts in a frying pan over a low heat for 1–2 minutes and keep turning them until they become brown.

6 Garnish with the reserved parsley, scatter the pine nuts over the top of the hummus and drizzle with olive oil, if using.

7 Serve with raw vegetables or wholemeal pitta bread.

Chicken Liver with Pomegranate Molasses

Kasabet Djaj Ma'a Debes Rumman

Liver is an acquired taste, but if you like liver, this is a great recipe for you. It's sometimes cooked with molasses or lemon and coriander.

SERVES 4

PREPARATION TIME
5 minutes

COOKING TIME
10 minutes

30ml olive oil
400g chicken liver, trimmed and cut into cubes
2–3 garlic cloves, crushed
½ tsp salt, plus extra to season
½ tsp ground black pepper
1 tbsp pomegranate molasses
25g pomegranate seeds
15g pistachios, roughly chopped (optional)

1 Heat the oil in a frying pan. Add the liver and fry for a few minutes until the liver pieces are slightly browned.

2 Add the garlic and fry for another 1 minute, then add the salt, pepper and molasses and cook for another 2–3 minutes.

3 Sprinkle the pomegranate seeds and pistachios, if using, over the top and serve hot with bread.

Fish with Onions and Tahini
Samack Tagen

Tahini is such an important ingredient throughout the Middle East, especially with fish, which is never served without tahini sauce. In some recipes, fish is even cooked in tahini.

SERVES 4

PREPARATION TIME
10 minutes

COOKING TIME
30 minutes

1 large onion (about 185g), halved and thinly sliced
20ml sunflower or corn oil
100g tahini
2 garlic cloves, crushed
1 tsp salt
Juice of 1–2 lemons (about 50ml)
300g white fillet, skinless fish, cut into cubes
15g toasted split almonds
10g toasted pine nuts
10g parsley, chopped, to garnish
Pinch of red chilli powder, to garnish
Lemon wedges, to serve

1 Sauté the onion in the oil over a medium to low heat for 15 minutes until golden.

2 Meanwhile, prepare the tahini sauce. Mix the tahini with the garlic, salt and lemon juice. When it becomes thick and fluffy, gradually add 350ml water until you've added it all. (This is much thinner than a normal tahini sauce because it will thicken while cooking.)

3 Add the sauce to the onion and keep stirring until it begins to boil. Turn the heat to low, simmer for 10 minutes and stir it occasionally. If it becomes too dry, add a little more water.

4 Add the fish and cook for another 5 minutes until the fish is cooked. At this stage the tahini will start to separate.

5 Turn out onto a serving dish. Spread the almonds and pine nuts over the top and garnish with chopped parsley and a sprinkle of chilli powder. Serve with lemon wedges.

Shrimps with Garlic and Coriander
Kraydis Mtabal

This is such a tasty starter and it's always available by the seafront. I often cook this at home for its fabulous flavour in very little time.

SERVES 4

PREPARATION TIME
5 minutes (less if the prawns are peeled)

COOKING TIME
10 minutes

COOK'S TIP
Make sure you don't overcook the shrimps as overcooking will turn them tough and chewy.

1 tbsp olive oil
3 garlic cloves, thinly sliced
1 red chilli, deseeded and chopped
250g shrimps or prawns, peeled
30g coriander, chopped
20ml lemon juice
½ tsp salt

1 Mix the olive oil, garlic and chilli together in a frying pan and fry over a medium heat for 2 minutes or until you begin to smell the garlic – make sure it doesn't brown. Stir in the shrimps and cook for 3–4 minutes until they are cooked through. (Check they are cooked by cutting 1 through the middle.)

2 Add the coriander and stir to coat the shrimps in it. Cook for 1 minute.

3 Finally, add the lemon juice and salt and continue to cook for another couple of minutes.

4 Serve hot with bread.

Avocado and Tahini Dip
Mtabal Avocado wa Tahini

This dip combines two super-healthy ingredients – avocados and tahini. It is rich and so quick and simple to make.

SERVES 4

PREPARATION TIME
10 minutes

COOKING TIME
None

Juice of 1 lemon (about 30ml)
2–3 garlic cloves, crushed
½ tsp salt
50g tahini
2 large avocados (about 300g), peeled,
  destoned and chopped
A few coriander leaves, to garnish

1 Prepare the tahini sauce by adding the lemon juice, garlic and salt to the tahini and mixing to thicken it.

2 Add about 50ml of cold water, a little at a time, and keep mixing until you have a creamy texture with no lumps. Add a little more water if it looks too thick. (It should be similar to double cream in thickness.)

3 Put the chopped avocadoes and tahini sauce in a bowl and mix well.

4 Garnish with a few coriander leaves and serve with toasted pitta bread or any other bread of your choice.

5

Simple Light Meals and Sides

Opposite:
Alex and Sami
preparing a spread
of light dishes.

Some of the dishes you'll find in this chapter can be made to keep in the fridge for tasty healthy snacks. Others can be served as light meals and many more can be sides to accompany main dishes, especially if you are planning a feast. It's hard to separate recipes into mains or sides because many of the recipes here are suitable as mains, especially if you are a vegetarian or vegan.

Soups are never served as a starter because they are filling and are served only as a light meal. The soups in this chapter are authentic, basic, tasty, filling and contain many nutrients.

The recipes here are quick and simple and mostly made with just a few ingredients that are available in any supermarket. They are mainly vegetarian or vegan with the exception of a couple of recipes with chicken and meat.

The Lebanese love plant-based food and it is always important to have vegetable sides, especially if the main dish is fish or meat.

Roasted Cauliflower with Tahini Sauce
Karnabeet Meshwi

Cauliflower is usually one of the vegetables added to mixed fried vegetables. Everyone loves fried cauliflower, even people who never liked it before are happy to eat it served in this way. When I put a full plate of it on the table, my grandchildren pick at it until it's all gone! For a healthier option, we choose roasting instead of frying.

SERVES 4

PREPARATION TIME
10 minutes

COOKING TIME
30–40 minutes

1 Preheat the oven to 200°C/Fan 180°C/ Gas 6. Rinse the cauliflower florets in cold water and place them on a baking tray while still wet. Sprinkle with the salt and drizzle with olive oil. Turn the florets with your hands to coat in the salt and oil.

2 Place the tray in the oven and bake the cauliflower for 30–40 minutes until brown.

3 Remove the cauliflower from the oven and transfer to a serving dish. Sprinkle with the pomegranate seeds and chopped parsley.

4 Serve with tahini sauce and lemon wedges for squeezing over the florets.

1 large cauliflower, separated into florets
1 tsp salt
2 tbsp olive oil
30g pomegranate seeds
5g parsley leaves, chopped
Tahini sauce, to serve (see page 241)
1 lemon, cut into wedges, to serve

Feta and Spinach Salad
Salata Sabanekh

Previously I wrote only authentic recipes. In this book I've added recipes that have a more modern approach, which has become very popular in Lebanese restaurants and cafés. I recently had this salad, which was tasty and packed with nutritional ingredients.

SERVES 4

PREPARATION TIME
10–15 minutes

COOKING TIME
none

COOK'S TIP
This salad may be served with small slices of roasted chicken, making an ideal way to use up leftover roast.

20g basil leaves
30ml olive oil
Juice of 1 lemon (about 30ml)
200g cherry tomatoes
50g baby spinach leaves
½ yellow pepper (about 50g), chopped
220g courgettes, spiralised or coarsely grated
2 avocados (about 200g), cut into cubes
220g feta cheese, cut into cubes
40g pine nuts
Salt

1 Finely chop the basil in a food processor, then add the oil and lemon juice and process to make a dressing.

2 Put the remaining ingredients, except the salt, into a salad bowl.

3 Add the basil dressing and season with salt. Mix the salad well and serve immediately.

Crushed Boiled Potatoes with Sumac Onions
Batata B Sumac

The tangy flavour of sumac with onions turns a few potatoes into a special and delicious addition to any meal. Sumac is becoming more and more easy to source in western supermarkets.

SERVES 4

PREPARATION TIME
5–10 minutes

COOKING TIME
20 minutes

1 Boil the potatoes with or without the skin, in salted water, for 20 minutes until they are cooked in the centre.

2 Meanwhile, add the onion to a frying pan together with the oil and fry it over a medium heat for about 10–15 minutes until softened and brown.

3 Add the sumac with ½ a teaspoon of salt and stir through with the onion.

4 Drain the potatoes and roughly crush them. Place them on a serving plate and spread the sumac and onion mixture over the top.

5 Sprinkle with the pine nuts, and garnish with parsley, if you like.

6 Serve with chicken, lamb or fish, or just add to a spread of dishes as a side dish.

1kg new potatoes
1 large onion (about 200g), sliced
40ml olive oil
2 tsp sumac
½ tsp salt, plus extra for boiling
1 tbsp toasted pine nuts (optional)
A little chopped parsley, to garnish (optional)

Freekeh (Green Wheat) and Chicken Soup

Shorba Djaj wa Freekeh

This soup is delicious and is a great success with the family. *Freekeh* is the main ingredient, so you can add the vegetables of your choice.

SERVES 4

PREPARATION TIME
15 minutes plus soaking

COOKING TIME
50 minutes

300g chicken breast fillet, cut into small cubes
1 tsp ground cinnamon
½ tsp ground black pepper
1 tsp Lebanese mixed spice (optional, see page 237)
2 bay leaves
1 tsp salt
220g carrots, sliced
1 large onion (about 250g), chopped
250g cooked chickpeas
150g courgettes, cut into cubes
80g freekeh (green wheat), rinsed and soaked for 20 minutes
A little chilli sauce – see page 231 (optional)

1 Boil the chicken pieces in 1 litre of water with the cinnamon, pepper, Lebanese mixed spice, if using, bay leaves and salt for 15 minutes.

2 Add the carrots and onion and boil over a medium heat for 10 minutes.

3 Add the chickpeas and courgettes and cook for 5 minutes more.

4 Add the *freekeh* and cook for another 15–20 minutes, adding more water if the soup looks too thick.

5 Serve immediately, stirring in a little chilli sauce, if you like (see page 231).

Open Spinach Pizza
Manoushi Sabanekh

My four-year-old grandson, Reuben, loves to help me cook. He once suggested that we make pizza with the spinach topping that we make for the spinach triangles (see page 205). To me, it's important to encourage kids to help and form healthy eating habits and enjoy healthy food.

MAKES 4

PREPARATION TIME
30 minutes,
plus rising time

COOKING TIME
10–15 minutes

300g bread flour, plus extra for rolling
2 tsp instant dried yeast
½ tsp salt
30ml olive oil
200ml warm water

FOR THE TOPPING
200g fresh spinach, coarsely chopped
1 onion (about 70g), finely chopped
30ml olive oil
2 tsp sumac
Juice of half a lemon (about 15ml)
1 tsp salt

1 Mix the flour, yeast and salt together well, then add the oil and rub it into the flour mix.

2 Gradually add the warm water and knead the mixture to form a smooth soft dough. Cover and rest the dough in a fairly warm place, leaving it to rise until doubled in size. It may take up to 2 hours, depending on the surrounding temperature.

3 Mix all the topping ingredients together and set aside.

4 Preheat the oven at 220°C/Fan 200°C/Gas 7. When the dough has risen, knock it back, then divide it into 4 pieces. Roll out each piece of dough on a floured surface to about ½cm thickness.

5 Squeeze out the juice from the spinach mixture, then spread equal quantities of the topping over each rolled piece of dough just before baking.

6 Put the *manoushi* (pizza) on a heated oven tray and bake for 10–15 minutes until the edges are partly brown and crispy. Serve warm or cold.

Common Lebanese Omelette
Egget Bayd

This is the traditional Lebanese omelette where the key ingredients are parsley and onions. Sometimes, when foraging in the springtime, country people make it with wild dill instead of parsley.

SERVES 4

PREPARATION TIME
10 minutes

COOKING TIME
10 minutes

COOK'S TIP
This omelette is delicious eaten cold and is perfect for picnics, wrapped in bread.

6 large eggs
½ tsp ground cinnamon
½ tsp salt
¼ tsp ground black pepper
1 onion (about 90g), finely chopped
40g parsley, finely chopped
30ml olive oil

1 Whisk the eggs in a bowl with the cinnamon, salt and pepper.

2 Add the onion and parsley and mix well.

3 In a frying pan, heat the oil over a medium heat and add the egg mixture. Cook for 5 minutes without stirring, then check if the bottom is browned. When the omelette is set on the top and the bottom is brown, either turn it over to brown on the other side or place the pan under the grill to brown the top.

4 Remove the omelette from the heat and serve in wedges with a green salad.

Mediterranean Vegetable Salad with Tahini Dressing
Salata Ma'a Tahini

This unique salad is always popular. You can vary the vegetables to suit your taste.

SERVES 4

PREPARATION TIME
15 minutes

COOKING TIME
30 minutes

300g cauliflower, separated into florets
150g broccoli, separated into florets
150g courgettes, cut into thick strips
1 aubergine (about 180g), cubed
170g potatoes, cubed
30ml olive oil
1 tsp salt, plus extra to season
3 garlic cloves, crushed
Juice of 1–2 lemons (about 50ml)
80g tahini
100g cos lettuce leaves, chopped
1 red pepper (about 90g), deseeded and chopped
6–8 radishes, sliced
1 small onion (about 50g), chopped
2 tsp sumac
10g toasted pine nuts, to serve

1 Preheat the oven to 200°C/Fan 180°C/Gas 6. Put the cauliflower, broccoli, courgettes, aubergines and potatoes on a baking tray. Sprinkle over the oil and salt and mix well.

2 Roast the vegetables in the oven for 30 minutes until cooked through. Remove them from the oven and leave to cool.

3 In a bowl, add the garlic and lemon juice to the tahini, season with a little salt and mix. When the tahini becomes thick and fluffy, add a little water a bit at a time and keep mixing until you have a light, creamy texture.

4 Put the roasted vegetables in a serving bowl, add the lettuce, pepper, radishes, onion and sumac, pour in the tahini mixture and mix together.

5 Sprinkle the pine nuts over the top and serve.

Vegetable Soup with Vermicelli
Showraba Khoudrae

Vermicelli pasta is commonly used in Lebanon in chicken or vegetable soups, and with rice. With the addition of vermicelli, soup becomes thick and filling, which is why soup is served as a light meal and never as a starter.

SERVES 4–6

PREPARATION TIME
10–15 minutes

COOKING TIME
35 minutes

40ml olive oil
1 large onion (about 250g), chopped
300g carrots, diced
300g white turnip, diced (optional)
300g tomatoes, chopped
300g courgettes, cut into cubes
1 large red, yellow or green pepper (about 200g), deseeded and chopped
1 tsp salt
1 tsp ground cinnamon
½ tsp ground black pepper
15g parsley, chopped
100g dried vermicelli, lightly crushed

1 Heat the oil in a pan over a medium heat, then add the onion and fry for about 5 minutes.

2 Stir in the carrots and turnip. Cook for 5 minutes.

3 Add the tomatoes, courgettes and pepper, stir to combine, and cook for another 5 minutes.

4 Add the salt, cinnamon and pepper, then top with water, cover the pan and cook for 10 minutes.

5 Reserving a little for the garnish, add the parsley and the vermicelli to the soup and cook for another 10 minutes until the vermicelli are cooked through.

6 Serve in bowls garnished with the reserved parsley and a little bread on the side.

Lemony Beans
Fasoulia Mtabaleh

This dish is most commonly made with chickpeas and sometimes with beans. Here I chose flageolet beans, but any kind will work. I included this recipe in this chapter because it's quick, simple to make, delicious and a filling light meal.

SERVES 4

PREPARATION TIME
10 minutes, plus soaking if using dried beans

COOKING TIME
50 minutes, if using dried beans

400g cooked flageolet beans or 200g dried
3 garlic cloves, crushed
50ml olive oil, plus extra to serve (optional)
1 tsp salt
Juice of 1–2 lemons (about 50ml)
5g parsley, chopped, to garnish
Lemon wedges, to serve

1 If using dried beans, soak the beans overnight and drain. Put the beans in a pan, cover with fresh water and bring to the boil over a high heat. Turn the heat down to low and simmer for about 50 minutes. Make sure the beans are well cooked and soft, then remove from the heat and drain. Keep warm while you prepare the dressing.

2 Prepare the dressing by mixing the garlic, oil, salt and lemon juice together in a bowl.

3 Put the cooked beans in a serving bowl, pour over the dressing and mix well. If using tinned beans, drain the water and heat in fresh boiling water for 2–3 minutes.

4 Add extra olive oil to the surface, if desired, and sprinkle with chopped parsley.

5 Serve warm with lemon wedges for squeezing over the top.

Lebanese Vegetable Fry-up with Tomato Sauce
Makali

When the Lebanese say they are having a fry-up it means a mixture of fried vegetables. Everyone loves it! Now, as more people avoid fried food, we tend to roast the vegetables instead.

SERVES 4

PREPARATION TIME
10 minutes

COOKING TIME
30 minutes

1 large aubergine (about 400g), sliced lengthways
400g courgettes, sliced
1 large red pepper (about 200g), deseeded and cut into 8 pieces
1 large green pepper (about 200g), deseeded and cut into 8 pieces
200g shallots, halved
30ml olive oil
Salt

FOR THE SAUCE
30ml olive oil
3 garlic cloves, crushed
2 green chillies, deseeded and sliced (optional)
500g tomatoes, chopped
1 tsp salt

1 Preheat the oven to 200°C/Fan 180°C/Gas 6. Place all the prepared vegetables on a baking tray, drizzle with the oil, sprinkle with a little salt and bake for 30 minutes or until all the vegetables are browned.

2 Meanwhile, prepare the sauce. Put the oil, garlic and chillies in a frying pan and fry over a medium heat for 1 minute. Don't let the garlic brown.

3 Add the tomatoes and salt. Reduce the heat to low and cook them for 5 minutes until slightly thickened.

4 Serve the roasted vegetables with the tomato sauce and bread.

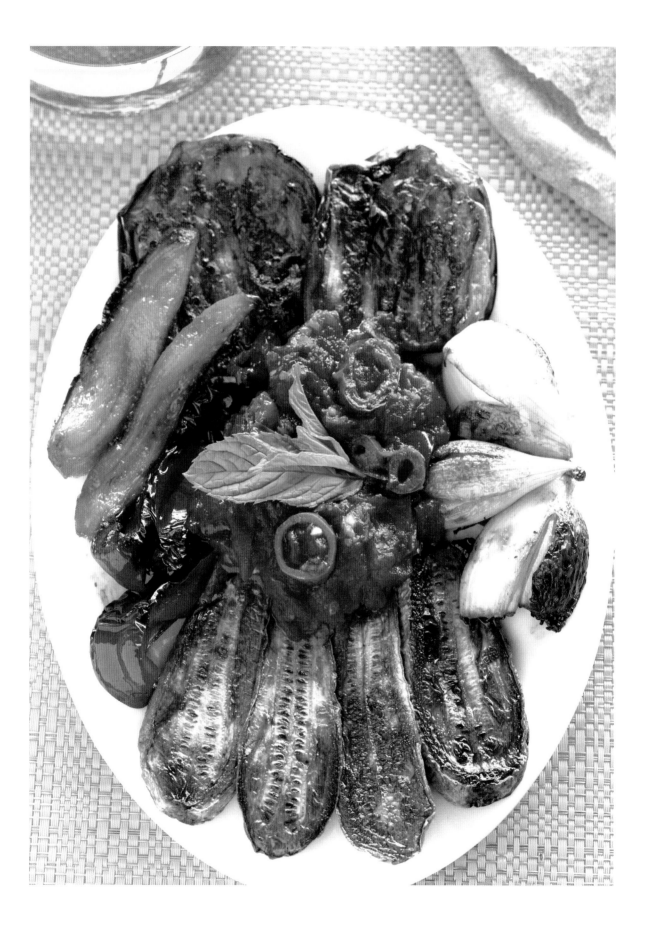

Sautéed Cabbage and Bulgur Wheat
Marshoushi

This peasant recipe is so tasty and simple to make. It's a satisfying light meal using only a few ingredients. Don't underestimate this dish for its simplicity. It is delicious.

SERVES 4

PREPARATION TIME
5 minutes

COOKING TIME
25–30 minutes

1 Rinse the bulgur wheat, drain and set aside. Bulgur wheat will soften enough just by being wet. If it turns soggy, too much water was left with it.

2 Heat the oil in a deep frying pan over a medium heat then add the onions and fry for about 5 minutes until softened.

3 Add the cabbage. Turn it with the onions and sauté for 10 minutes.

4 Add the bulgur wheat with about 300ml of water. Add the salt, pepper and cayenne pepper, if using, and mix all the ingredients together.

5 Cover and simmer over a low heat for 10–15 minutes.

6 Serve with either a yogurt salad or any other salad of your choice. (See the salad chapter.)

130g coarse bulgur wheat (burghul)
40ml olive oil
2 red onions (about 300g), chopped
650g sweetheart or savoy cabbage,
  sliced lengthways
1 tsp salt
½ tsp ground black pepper
½ tsp cayenne pepper (optional)

Roasted Courgettes with Minted Yogurt
Coosa Blaban

Because of the variety of dishes we can make using courgettes and it being one of our favourite vegetables, there are always some in the fridge to use for a quick light meal. This is a tasty, refreshing snack especially in the summer.

SERVES 4

PREPARATION TIME
10 minutes

COOKING TIME
20 minutes

500g courgettes, sliced
20ml olive oil
200g natural yogurt (see page 236)
3 garlic cloves, crushed
1 tsp dried mint
½ tsp salt, plus extra to season
½ tsp sumac

1 Preheat the oven to 200°C/Fan 180°C/Gas 6. Place the courgettes on a baking tray, drizzle over the oil and season with salt. Roast them in the oven for 20 minutes until a little brown.

2 Remove the courgettes from the oven and allow them to cool. Transfer them to a serving dish

3 Mix the yogurt, garlic, mint and salt together, then pour the mixture over the roasted courgettes.

4 Sprinkle the sumac over the top. Serve as a side dish, or just by itself with bread.

Roasted Aubergines with Pitta and Garlic Yogurt
Fetteh Batingane

Fetteh is made with a number of different ingredients, but whatever it's made with it always includes pitta croutons and is topped with garlic yogurt. This is what makes the fetteh. It is light, tasty and quick to make.

SERVES 4

PREPARATION TIME
10 minutes

COOKING TIME
15 minutes

COOK'S TIP
Fetteh is delicious made also with chickpeas.

2 aubergines (about 300g), sliced lengthways
2 tbsp olive oil
150g Lebanese or pitta bread
2 garlic cloves, crushed
500g natural yogurt (see page 236)
20g pomegranate seeds
20g toasted pine nuts
A few mint leaves, chopped
Salt

1 Rub a little salt on the aubergines and drizzle with olive oil.

2 Griddle, roast or brown the aubergines on both sides in a frying pan. At the same time, toast the bread to brown it and break it into small pieces. Toast the bread for roughly 3 minutes or less so it can brown and then break into small pieces. This bread is so thin that, when browned on one side, it tends to brown the other side, too.

3 Arrange the aubergines on a serving dish, then add the toasted bread.

4 Mix the garlic with a little salt and the yogurt, then pour the mixture over the aubergines and bread.

5 Sprinkle the pomegranate seeds, toasted pine nuts and chopped mint over the top.

6 Serve immediately. The bread will get soggy if left for too long.

Kafta Toasties
Arayes

Kafta is a simple mixture of minced lamb or beef with parsley and onions. Because of its popularity in the Middle East, it is served in so many different ways. This recipe is quick, simple and makes a delicious light meal or can be served with the maza.

SERVES 4

PREPARATION TIME
5–10 minutes

COOKING TIME
10 minutes

300g minced lamb
20g parsley, finely chopped
1 small to medium onion (about 100g), grated or finely chopped
½ tsp ground cinnamon
½ tsp salt
¼ tsp ground black pepper
4 Lebanese flatbreads or pitta bread (see page 234)
A little oil, for brushing

FOR THE GARNISH (OPTIONAL)
A little chopped parsley
A few cherry tomatoes

1 Preheat the oven to 200ºC/Fan 180ºC/Gas 6. Mix the mince with the parsley, onion, cinnamon, salt and pepper, so all the ingredients are combined and hold together.

2 Split the loaves open and divide the kafta into 4 portions. Evenly spread 1 portion on 1 side of the split loaf and fold the other half over so the kafta is sandwiched in the middle.

3 Place the loaves on a baking tray, brush with a little oil and cook in the oven for 10–15 minutes until the bread is crispy and slightly brown.

4 Garnish with parsley and cherry tomatoes, if using. Serve hot with a hummus dip and natural yogurt on the side.

Red Lentil Soup
Shorbat Adas

At school, we were served this lentil soup and fresh fruit every day, mainly because it's low cost, nutritious and tasty.

SERVES 4

PREPARATION TIME
5 minutes

COOKING TIME
35 minutes

COOK'S TIP
You can add chopped tomatoes, carrots and peppers too, if you like. Sometimes, roasted red peppers are chopped and added to the basic soup.

350g orange split lentils, rinsed and drained
50ml olive oil
1 tsp cumin seeds
2 onions (about 300g), diced
½ tsp ground cinnamon
1 tsp salt
Juice of 1 lemon (about 30ml), optional, or lemon wedges to serve
Pitta bread, toasted

1 Bring 1 litre of water to the boil and add the rinsed lentils. Cook over a medium heat for 25 minutes until the lentils look mushy. Add more water if needed. Remember, this is a thick soup.

2 While the lentils are cooking, heat the oil in a frying pan over a medium heat. Stir in the cumin seeds and cook for 1 minute, then add the onions and fry for about 10 minutes until they are golden brown. When the lentils are ready stir the onions into the pan.

3 Cook the soup for another 10 minutes and add the cinnamon, salt and lemon juice, if using.

4 Serve with toasted pitta bread and, if you haven't used lemon juice, lemon wedges on the side.

Freekeh (Green Wheat) with Peppers and Tomatoes
Freekeh Ma'a Banadoura

This tasty grain is very popular in certain parts of Lebanon and can be cooked in so many different ways or used as a substitute to rice. It is rich in protein and fibre.

SERVES 4

PREPARATION TIME
10 minutes, plus
soaking

COOKING TIME
35 minutes

30ml olive oil
2 onions (about 250g), chopped
2–3 garlic cloves, chopped
1 large red pepper (about 140g), deseeded
  and chopped into chunks
1 large yellow pepper (about 140g), deseeded
  and chopped into chunks
1 tsp salt
½ tsp allspice (pimento)
½ tsp ground cinnamon
450g tomatoes, chopped
300g freekeh, rinsed and soaked
  for 20 minutes
Chilli powder (optional)

1 Heat the oil in a large saucepan, add the onions and garlic and fry for 10 minutes over a medium heat until the vegetables are slightly golden. Add the peppers and fry for another 5 minutes, then stir in the salt, allspice and cinnamon and cook for 30 seconds.

2 Add the tomatoes, cover the pan and simmer over a low heat for 5 minutes.

3 Add the *freekeh* and a little water just to cover the surface. Bring to the boil, cover the pan again and simmer over a low heat for 15 minutes until all the water has evaporated.

4 Transfer to a serving dish, sprinkle with chilli powder, if using, and serve with natural yogurt and/or a salad.

The Healthy Lebanese Family Cookbook

Dandelion Leaves with Crispy Onions and Lemons
Hindbeh Bzeit

This extremely popular dish is often served with the maza spread or on its own. Many people love this dish, even without the knowledge of its super nutritional value. Dandelion leaves are cultivated all year round, but country people go foraging to pick them wild. The dish is rich in vitamins A and C and in calcium and has twice as much iron as spinach. Above all, it is delicious.

SERVES 4

PREPARATION TIME
15 minutes

COOKING TIME
30 minutes

60ml olive oil
2 large onions (about 370g), halved and
  thinly sliced
700g dandelion leaves (hindbeh), rinsed,
  drained and chopped
2 garlic cloves, sliced
1 tsp salt
Juice of 1 lemon (about 30ml), plus 2 lemons
  cut into wedges to serve

1 Put 40ml of the oil in a frying pan over a medium heat. Add the onions and fry for 10 minutes until they are light brown. At the same time, place the dandelion leaves in a separate pan, cover and steam them over a medium to low heat. The leaves will steam in their own juice to dry out.

2 Add half the browned onions to the pan with the leaves, along with the garlic, salt and lemon juice. Allow everything to cook for another 20 minutes until most of the moisture has evaporated.

3 Fry the remaining onions for another 5 minutes until they are brown and crispy. Remove from the heat and spread the crispy onions over kitchen paper.

4 Add the remaining oil to the dandelion leaves and stir through.

5 Turn the hindbeh out onto a serving plate and sprinkle the crispy onions over the top. Serve cold with flatbread and lemon wedges.

Roasted Mediterranean Vegetables with Zaatar and Sumac
Khoudra Meshwiyeh Ma'a Zaatar

This super bake is delicious and preserves most of the vitamins contained in the roasted vegetables. You can serve it as a side dish, on its own, or with any meat you choose.

SERVES 4

PREPARATION TIME
10–15 minutes

COOKING TIME
40 minutes

250g cauliflower, cut into small florets
1 red pepper, deseeded and cut into large pieces
1 orange pepper, deseeded and cut into large pieces
2 red onions (about 250g), cut into quarters
250g courgettes, sliced into rounds
200g carrots, cut into strips
5 garlic cloves
1 tsp salt
2 tsp zaatar or thyme
1 tbsp sumac
30ml olive oil
Tahini sauce (see page 241), to serve

1 Preheat the oven to 220°C/Fan 200°C/ Gas 7. Put all the vegetables and the whole garlic cloves on a baking tray and rub in the salt, zaatar or thyme and sumac.

2 Add the oil and mix well.

3 Roast the vegetables in the oven for 20 minutes.

4 Remove the tray from the oven and turn the vegetables with a wooden spoon before returning them to the oven. Roast the vegetables for another 20 minutes until they are a little crispy.

5 Serve with bread, and tahini sauce (see page 241) drizzled over the top.

Chickpeas with Tomatoes and Coriander
Hummus Bzeit

Pulses feature often in Lebanese cooking. This high-protein dish is simple and tasty. I always make extra to keep in the fridge, ready to enjoy as a snack.

SERVES 4

PREPARATION TIME
10 minutes

COOKING TIME
30 minutes

1 Fry the onion in 30ml of the oil over a medium heat for 10 minutes. Add the garlic and fry for another 1 minute, then add the chilli and cumin. Stir together for 1 minute.

2 Add the chopped tomatoes, salt and diluted tomato purée. Stir and cook for 5 minutes.

3 Add the cooked chickpeas, turn gently, cover the pan and simmer over a low heat for 10 minutes.

4 Reserving a little coriander for the garnish, add the rest to the chickpeas, gently stir and cook for another 3 minutes.

5 Remove from the heat and add the remaining oil.

6 Garnish with the reserved coriander and serve with flatbread.

1 large onion (about 200g), chopped
50ml olive oil
4 garlic cloves, chopped
½ tsp chilli powder (optional)
2 tsp ground cumin
170g tomatoes, chopped
1 tsp salt
40g tomato purée diluted in 150ml water
360g cooked chickpeas (see p39)
50g coriander, chopped

Freekeh (Green Wheat) Salad
Salata Freekeh

I made up this salad in order to use *freekeh* in more dishes. Apart from enjoying its flavour and the texture, I feel good after eating it. This salad works really well on its own or with kebabs and chicken served on the side.

SERVES 4

PREPARATION TIME
15 minutes

COOKING TIME
20 minutes

1 Rinse the *freekeh* well and then soak it for 20 minutes.

2 Drain the water, add the salt and cover it with boiling water until the water reaches to about 2cm above the *freekeh*. Bring the water to the boil, cover, turn the heat down to low and simmer for 20 minutes until all the water has evaporated. Remove from the heat and allow to cool.

3 Once cool, add the peppers, mint, parsley, lemon juice and oil, taste for seasoning and mix well.

4 Transfer the salad to a serving plate and sprinkle the pomegranate seeds over the top.

5 Serve as a side dish or on its own as a salad.

150g freekeh
½ tsp salt
1 red pepper (about 75g), deseeded and chopped
1 green pepper (about 75g), deseeded and chopped
5g mint, chopped
30g parsley, chopped
Juice of 1 lemon (about 30ml)
30ml olive oil
30g pomegranate seeds

Lentil and Rainbow Chard Soup
Adas Bhamod

This unique, tasty and healthy soup is an absolute favourite of mine since childhood and therefore, it's in all my books. I really believe everyone should try it and I am sure you will love it as much as I do.

SERVES 4

PREPARATION TIME
10 minutes

COOKING TIME
1 hour

COOK'S TIP
Use either green or rainbow chard, whichever is available.

250g green or brown lentils, rinsed
1.5 litres boiling water
50ml olive oil
1 large onion (about 250g), chopped
500g chard stalks and leaves, chopped
(or spinach if chard is unavailable)
Juice of 2–3 lemons (about 50ml)
1–2 tsp salt
2 tsp sumac

1 Put the lentils in a pan with the boiling water. Cover the pan and simmer the lentils over a low heat for 40 minutes.

2 Meanwhile, put half the oil in a frying pan, add the onions and fry for 10–15 minutes until light brown. Set aside.

3 When the lentils have been cooking for 40 minutes, add the onions, chard and lemon juice and cook for 15 minutes more.

4 When the lentils are well cooked, add the salt and cook for another 2–3 minutes. (Always add the salt after the pulses are well cooked to avoid them remaining hard.) Turn off the heat and stir in the remaining oil.

5 Serve with pitta bread and more lemon if you like and sprinkle with sumac.

Peasant Lemony Courgettes
Treedeh

Because courgettes are so bland, they are a great basic ingredient for bringing out other flavours. This dish is often cooked in the mountains where there are too many courgettes to be used.

SERVES 4

PREPARATION TIME
10 minutes

COOKING TIME
20 minutes

COOK'S TIP
Use 2 tsp of dried mint if fresh mint is unavailable.

40ml olive oil
1 large onion (about 250g), finely chopped
650g courgettes, chopped
Juice of 1 lemon (about 30ml)
3–4 garlic cloves, crushed
1 tsp salt
20g fresh mint, chopped, plus a few extra leaves, chopped, to garnish
100g pitta bread, toasted and broken into small pieces

1 Heat 20ml of the oil in a frying pan over a medium heat, add the onion and fry for 10 minutes.

2 Add the courgettes and continue to cook for another 10 minutes until the courgettes are cooked and there is no moisture in the pan.

3 Meanwhile, make a sauce by mixing the lemon juice, crushed garlic, salt and chopped mint together.

4 When the courgettes are ready, add the sauce to the pan and turn to combine over a medium heat for a few seconds.

5 Remove from the heat and stir through the remaining olive oil.

6 Transfer to a serving dish, sprinkle over the toasted pitta and the extra chopped mint.

Quinoa Tabbouleh
Taboulet Quinoae

Quinoa is a high-protein plant food and many of those conscious about their health prefer it. Traditional tabbouleh is usually made with a small amount of bulgur wheat but here quinoa is the dominant ingredient. It tastes completely different from the traditional tabbouleh, but is richer in protein.

SERVES 4

PREPARATION TIME
20 minutes

COOKING TIME
20 minutes

130g quinoa, rinsed and drained
400ml boiling water
1½ tsp salt
100g flat-leaf parsley, chopped
15g mint, chopped
450g tomatoes, chopped
1 onion (about 120g), chopped
1 yellow or orange pepper (about 120g), diced
1 red chilli (about 20g), deseeded and sliced
  (optional)
Juice of 1–2 lemons (about 50ml)
30ml olive oil

1 Place the quinoa in a saucepan with the boiling water and ½ a teaspoon of salt. Place over a medium heat and boil for 5 minutes, then cover the pan, turn the heat down to low and cook for another 15 minutes, making sure all the water has evaporated. Allow it to cool.

2 Meanwhile, reserving a few slices of chilli to garnish, put all the remaining ingredients in a mixing bowl and mix thoroughly. Add the cooled quinoa and mix again.

3 Turn out the tabbouleh onto a serving dish and garnish with sliced chilli, if desired.

Spinach and Feta Cheese Bread
Fatayer

This recipe, with the lovely combination of spinach and feta cheese, has been used in so many different cuisines. It's made in various sizes depending on the occasion.

SERVES 4

PREPARATION TIME
15 minutes plus rinsing time

COOKING TIME
30 minutes

FOR THE DOUGH
200g bread flour, plus extra for rolling
2 tsp instant dried yeast
½ tsp salt
About 200ml slightly warm water

FOR THE FILLING
20ml olive oil, plus extra for oiling and brushing
1 onion (about 120g), chopped
2 garlic cloves, chopped
400g spinach, roughly chopped
100g tomatoes, deseeded and chopped
200g feta cheese, crumbled
10g sesame seeds

1 Make the dough, following the instructions for the Lebanese flatbread (see page 234).

2 To make the filling, mix the oil and onion together and fry over a medium heat for 10 minutes until softened and slightly golden.

3 Add the garlic and stir with the onions for 2 minutes, then add the spinach and tomatoes and cook for 5 minutes. Remove from the heat and allow to cool, then mix in the cheese.

4 Preheat the oven to 220°C/Fan 200°C/ Gas 7. Divide the dough into 2, 3 or 4 balls, depending on the size you want. Roll the dough out very thinly on a floured surface, so it is almost transparent. Divide the filling, placing equal amounts in the middle of each piece of dough. Gently raise the edges of the dough until you can squeeze them together centrally to seal and enclose the filling. Cut off any extra dough.

5 Place each filled piece of dough on a well-oiled baking tray, sealed side down and flatten with your hands.

6 Brush the surface of each round with oil and sprinkle sesame seeds over the top.

7 Bake for 15 minutes in the oven until golden. Then remove and serve warm with lemon wedges.

6

Family Main Dishes

Opposite:
A family get together
for lunch.

In this chapter there are many varied and affordable dishes to suit every taste. There are recipes with chicken, meat, fish, as well as vegetarian dishes. The latter are mostly suitable for vegans too. They are easy to prepare with ingredients available in supermarkets, including all the Mediterranean varieties of vegetables that are often used in these recipes.

Lebanese food is known to be one of the healthiest in the world and in this book I've made the recipes even healthier and given them a more modern approach. The majority of the dishes use more vegetables and less meat. Lebanese people are accustomed to having very little meat in their diet. Meat and chicken are usually eaten on average once a week and only a small amount of it. We are basically a vegetable-loving nation and that's how we were brought up.

In Lebanon, fish is always more popular than meat and is easily available, fresh and locally caught. Living in the mountains, further from the sea, the fish van will come to your door a minimum of three times a week. You will find several fish dishes in this chapter and all can be easily prepared with simple ingredients.

Many dishes are served with plain or aromatic rice, mainly Lebanese rice cooked with vermicelli. This food is always popular with young children. When my children were very young and invited their friends over, our little guests always requested Lebanese food for dinner. I hope your children will love it too.

Chicken Pieces with Zaatar and Sumac

Djaj Be Zaatar Wa Sumac

Zaatar and sumac are such basic ingredients, but I never believed that these could be such a great combination with chicken until I tried it. Above all, this dish requires very little effort.

SERVES 4

PREPARATION TIME
15 minutes, plus
marinating time

COOKING TIME
50 minutes

1 In a large bowl, mix the onions, garlic, allspice, cinnamon, pepper, sumac, zaatar and olive oil to make a marinade.

2 Add the chicken pieces to the marinade and mix well to coat. Leave to marinate in the fridge for at least 1 hour.

3 Preheat the oven to 200°C/Fan 180°C/Gas 6. Add the salt just before you are about to cook the chicken and spread out the marinated chicken in an ovenproof dish, pouring the onion marinade over the top. Sprinkle over the sesame seeds.

4 Cook in the oven for 50 minutes or until the chicken is cooked through. Remove the chicken from the oven and cover with foil to rest and to absorb moisture before serving.

5 Scatter the pomegranate seeds over the top and garnish with the chopped parsley.

2 large onions (about 400g), halved and sliced
5–6 garlic cloves, sliced
1 tsp allspice
1 tsp ground cinnamon
½ tsp ground black pepper
1 tbsp sumac
½ tbsp zaatar
75ml olive oil
1.5kg free-range chicken, cut into small pieces
  and skin removed
1 tsp salt
10g sesame seeds
20g pomegranate seeds
A little parsley, chopped, to garnish

6 Serve with plain or saffron rice (see page 191) and Armenian mixed salad (see page 233).

Grilled Marinated Fish
Samack Tawouk

Fish is rarely served without tahini sauce on the side, but some fish recipes require the fish to be cooked with the tahini sauce instead. This recipe was my first attempt to marinate chunky cubes of fish in tahini to make a kebab-style fish. It is delicious and works brilliantly.

SERVES 4

PREPARATION TIME
10 minutes plus
marinating

COOKING TIME
10 minutes

100g tahini
Juice of 1 lemon (about 30ml)
1 tsp salt
½ tsp white pepper
4 garlic cloves, crushed
1kg skinless white fish fillet (cod or monkfish),
  cut into large cubes
2 red or yellow peppers (about 250g),
  deseeded and cut into large pieces
300g small vine tomatoes
5g parsley, chopped, to garnish
2 lemons, cut into wedges

1 In a large bowl mix together the tahini, lemon juice, salt, white pepper and garlic to make a marinade. Keep mixing until the marinade becomes thick and fluffy. Add about 20ml of water and keep mixing until you have a smooth, creamy sauce.

2 Add the fish pieces to the marinade and turn to coat. Leave to marinate in the fridge for 2–3 hours.

3 Skewer the fish pieces and peppers. If using wooden skewers, be sure to soak them in water first. Cook the fish on a high temperature on a barbecue or grill for 10 minutes. Overcooking the fish will make it dry and chewy.

4 At the same time, barbecue or grill the tomatoes.

5 Garnish the dish with the chopped parsley.

6 Serve with saffron rice (see page 233), a salad of your choice and lemon wedges.

Kafta with Aubergine Bake
Kafta Ma'a Batingane

This dish is commonly cooked with potatoes. Since the first time I tried it with aubergines, I've never looked back and it has remained one of my favourites.

SERVES 4

PREPARATION TIME
10 minutes

COOKING TIME
45 minutes

30ml olive oil
2 large aubergines (about 600g), sliced 2cm thick, horizontally
500g minced lamb or beef, or a mixture of both
1 small onion (about 90g), finely chopped
40g parsley, finely chopped, reserving a little for the garnish
1 tsp ground cinnamon
½ tsp ground black pepper
450g tomatoes, sliced 1cm thick
70g tomato purée diluted in 300ml warm water and mixed with ½ tsp salt
20g roasted almonds
30g roasted pine nuts
Salt

1 Preheat the oven to 220°C/Fan 200°C/ Gas 7. Drizzle 10ml of the oil over the aubergine slices and season with a little salt. Place the aubergines on a baking sheet and roast in the oven for 20 minutes until brown.

2 Meanwhile, in a bowl combine the minced meat, onion, parsley, cinnamon and pepper. Season with salt and mix well with your hands.

3 Divide and shape the meat mixture into 8 evenly sized patties, then place them in a deep oven dish. Bake the balls in the oven for 10 minutes until the meat is part cooked.

4 Remove the dish from the oven and lay the cooked aubergine slices over the meat. Add the tomato slices in another layer and pour the diluted tomato purée over the top. Cook in the oven for 25 minutes at the same temperature as above.

5 Serve with basmati or vermicelli rice (see page 239), add the almonds and pine nuts and sprinkle with parsley to garnish.

Fish with Spinach and Chilli
Yakhnet Samack wa Sbanekh

Whenever I feel like eating a fish dish with rice, this is the one I go for. It is tasty, light and can be cooked in just a short time with little effort.

SERVES 4–6

PREPARATION TIME
10 minutes

COOKING TIME
40 minutes

50ml olive oil
2 medium onions (about 300g), chopped
5 garlic cloves, chopped
1 tsp ground red chilli powder
2 tsp paprika
1 heaped tsp salt
1kg white fish fillets, skinned and
  cut into cubes
1kg fresh or frozen spinach, roughly chopped
150g tomatoes, chopped

1 Heat the oil in a large, deep, lidded frying pan over a medium heat. Add the onions and fry for 10 minutes. Add the garlic and continue frying for another 1 minute.

2 Add the chilli, paprika and salt. Stir for 1 minute, then add the fish pieces and gently coat with the onion mixture.

3 Add the spinach and tomatoes, cover the pan and simmer for 10 minutes until the spinach is well reduced. Gently turn the spinach with the fish and onions and cook for another 10 minutes.

4 Uncover the pan and simmer for 5 minutes to reduce the liquid from the spinach.

5 Serve with plain basmati rice.

Bulgur Wheat with Mixed Vegetables
Burghul Bkhudra

I've always been a big fan of burghul, whichever way it is prepared. This dish is quick and simple and you can add any vegetable you like.

SERVES 4–6

PREPARATION TIME
15 minutes

COOKING TIME
35–40 minutes

30ml olive oil
1 large onion (about 150g), chopped
3–4 garlic cloves, crushed
1 heaped tsp ground cumin
1 tsp salt
½ tsp ground black pepper
100g carrots, diced
1 small–medium green or red pepper (about 80g),
  halved, deseeded and sliced
120g courgettes, chopped
85g green beans, trimmed and cut to
  4cm-long pieces
500g tomatoes, chopped
1 green or red chilli, chopped (optional)
200g coarse bulgur wheat (burghul),
  rinsed and drained

1 Heat the oil in a large, deep, lidded frying pan over a medium heat. Add the onions and fry for 10 minutes. Add the garlic and continue frying for another 1 minute.

2 Add the cumin, salt and pepper and stir for 1 minute.

3 Add the carrots, peppers, courgettes, beans, tomatoes, and chilli, if using, cover the pan and simmer over a low heat for 15 minutes until tender. The vegetables should cook in their own juices.

4 Add the bulgur wheat, mix well with the vegetables and cook for another 10 minutes. If you think it needs a little more moisture to cook, just add 50ml of water.

5 Serve with natural yogurt or cabbage salad (see page 192).

Aubergines Filled with Minced Meat
Sheikh El Mehshi

I loved this dish as a very young child and still do. It has a fabulous combination of flavours, and is equally suitable to serve as a family dinner or at a dinner party.

SERVES 4–6

PREPARATION TIME
10 minutes

COOKING TIME
1 hour

3 large aubergines (about 800g),
    cut in half lengthwise
30ml olive oil, plus extra for rubbing
1 tsp salt, plus extra for rubbing
1 large onion (about 200g), chopped
400g minced lamb or beef
1 tsp ground cinnamon
½ tsp allspice
½ tsp ground black pepper
250g tomatoes, chopped
80g tomato purée, diluted in 400ml water
15g toasted pine nuts, to garnish
10g chopped parsley, to garnish

1 Preheat the oven to 200°C/Fan 180°C/Gas 6. Rub the aubergines with oil and a little salt, place them on a baking tray and bake them for 15 minutes until brown.

2 Meanwhile, heat 30ml of oil in a frying pan, add the onion and fry over a medium heat for 2–3 minutes to brown. Add the minced meat and fry for another 5 minutes until the meat is browned. Stir in the cinnamon, allspice and pepper then remove from the heat and set aside.

3 When the aubergines are ready, slit each half in the middle and push the flesh to the sides to make space for the filling. Place the aubergine halves in an ovenproof dish and fill each half with an equal amount of the mince and onion mixture. Spread the chopped tomatoes over the top of each half, add the 1 teaspoon of salt to the diluted tomato purée and pour the mixture over the top of the aubergines.

4 Return the aubergines to the oven and bake for 30–40 minutes until the sauce has thickened.

5 Garnish with toasted pine nuts and chopped parsley and serve with Lebanese vermicelli rice (see page 239) or saffron rice (see page 233).

Stuffed Cabbage Leaves
Mehshi Malfoof

Stuffed vegetables, such as baby aubergines, courgettes, peppers and vine leaves, are very popular throughout the Middle East. Cabbage is a favourite and is easily available. This dish is always a favourite with my family.

SERVES 4

PREPARATION TIME
35 minutes, plus soaking time

COOKING TIME
40–45 minutes

450g cabbage leaves (sweet heart or flat cabbage)
1 litre boiling water

FOR THE FILLING
300g risotto or pudding rice, rinsed and soaked for 30 minutes
50ml olive oil
Juice of 2–3 lemons (about 50ml)
200g cooked chickpeas
100g flat-leaf parsley, chopped
30g mint leaves, chopped
150g spring onions including leaves, chopped
500g tomatoes, chopped
6 garlic cloves
500ml hot water
1tsp of salt, to taste

FOR THE GARNISH (OPTIONAL)
A small handful of pomegranate seeds
1 lemon, sliced
A few mint leaves

1 Blanche the cabbage leaves in the boiling water for 3 minutes to soften. Place them in a sieve to drain.

2 Drain the rice, add 30ml of the oil and half the lemon juice, then add the remaining filling ingredients, except the garlic, and mix well.

3 Cut each cabbage leaf in half or quarter if large, removing and reserving the stalk from the middle.

4 On each cabbage leaf, place 2 teaspoons of the filling in a line, fold the cabbage over the filling and roll up firmly to enclose it completely.

5 Line the bottom of a saucepan with the reserved cabbage stalks then lay the rolled cabbage leaves over the top with the garlic cloves scattered in between the layers.

6 Pour the 500ml of hot water over the top with a sprinkle of salt to taste and the remaining lemon juice. Cook over a medium heat for 40–45 minutes.

7 Remove from the heat and drizzle the remaining oil over the top before transferring everything, including the cabbage stalks, to a serving dish. Serve hot or cold.

8 An optional garnish of pomegranate seeds, lemon slices and mint leaves can be added.

Potato Stew in Rich Tomato Sauce
Yakhnet Batata

Potato dishes are very popular as they can be easily prepared in a variety of ways. This lovely dish can be enjoyed by all the family, especially children. You can leave out the meat if you prefer.

SERVES 4

PREPARATION TIME
15–20 minutes

COOKING TIME
1 hour

2 onions (about 250g), chopped
30ml olive oil
400g beef, cut into cubes
4 garlic cloves, crushed
1 tsp ground cinnamon
½ tsp allspice (optional)
½ tsp ground black pepper
70g tomato purée
1 litre hot water
1kg new potatoes, peeled
1 tsp salt
40g coriander leaves and stalks, chopped

1 Put the onions and oil in a saucepan and fry over a medium heat for about 5–10 minutes until the onions are golden brown.

2 Add the meat and fry with the onions for 2–3 minutes. Add the garlic, cinnamon, allspice, if using, and pepper and stir with the meat and onions for another 2 minutes.

3 Add the tomato purée and hot water. When the water starts to boil turn the heat down a little, cover the pan and cook for 30 minutes. Add the potatoes and salt and cook for another 15 minutes. Now the meat should be tender, the potatoes well cooked and the sauce rich.

4 If the sauce looks too thick, add a bit more water. Saving a little coriander for the garnish, add the coriander and cook for another 5 minutes. Garnish with the reserved coriander.

5 Serve with plain or Lebanese vermicelli rice (see page 239).

Grilled Kafta and Peppers
Kafta Meshwiyeh

This last-minute meal can be prepared and cooked in less than 30 minutes and is suitable for all the family and guests. Whether you are grilling or barbecuing, always serve the *kafta* with dips like hummus or yogurt salad.

SERVES 4

PREPARATION TIME
5–10 minutes

COOKING TIME
15 minutes

700g minced lamb
1 onion (about 140g), finely chopped or grated
80g flat-leaf parsley, finely chopped
1 tsp salt
1 tsp ground cinnamon
½ tsp ground black pepper
1 green, 1 yellow, 1 red pepper (about 300g
  in total), deseeded and cut into quarters
300g vine tomatoes
½ tbsp olive oil

1 Using your hands, in a bowl combine the mince, onion, parsley, salt, cinnamon and black pepper.

2 Divide the mixture into equal-sized 8–10 balls, then press each between your hands to form them into burger shapes, each about 1cm thick.

3 Meanwhile, drizzle the peppers and tomatoes with the oil and place them under a hot grill. After 5 minutes, place the *kafta* under the grill with the vegetables and cook for 2–3 minutes.

4 Turn both the kafta, peppers and tomatoes once and roughly grill for another 5 minutes to brown all over.

5 Serve with Lebanese-style potato salad (see page 193), Lebanese flatbread (see page 234) and/or Arabian salad (see page 185).

Freekeh (Green Wheat) with Caramelised Shallots and Chickpeas

Freekeh Ma'a Hummus

This economical dish is frequently cooked in families with a low income, but besides being inexpensive to make, we love it and it contains a huge amount of protein and fibre.

SERVES 4

PREPARATION TIME
5 minutes

COOKING TIME
About 30 minutes

250g shallots
30ml olive oil
3 garlic cloves, chopped
1 tsp salt
½ tsp ground black pepper
1 heaped tsp ground cinnamon
1 tsp mixed spices (see page 237)
2 tsp ground cumin
500g cooked chickpeas (see page 39)
20g coriander, chopped
300g freekeh, rinsed and soaked in cold water

1 Peel the shallots and cut them in halves if large. Place them in a pan with the oil and fry them over a medium heat for 5–10 minutes until slightly browned.

2 Add the garlic and stir for 1 minute, then add the salt, pepper and all the spices. Stir for another 1 minute.

3 Add the chickpeas and chopped coriander and turn to mix everything together.

4 Drain the *freekeh*, mix it with the chickpeas and top with water to cover it by 1cm. Bring to the boil and continue to boil for 2–3 minutes until the water is level with the *freekeh*. Turn down the heat to low, cover and allow to simmer for about 20 minutes until all the water has evaporated.

5 Serve with natural yogurt (as is traditional), or a salad of your choice, if you prefer.

Chicken and Aubergine Bake
Batingane Ma'a Djaj

This tasty dish is so simple to prepare. Sometimes potatoes are used instead of aubergines or sometimes both. All versions are delicious.

SERVES 4

PREPARATION TIME
10 minutes

COOKING TIME
40–50 minutes

20ml olive oil, plus extra for frying
1 large aubergine (about 350g), sliced into
  1.5cm-thick rounds
1 large onion (about 200g), sliced
3–4 garlic cloves, sliced
1 tsp ground cinnamon
½ tsp ground black pepper
½ tsp mixed spices (see page 237)
4 skinless, boneless organic chicken breasts
  (about 100g each)
300g tomatoes, sliced
100g tomato purée diluted in 400ml water
1 tsp salt
A little chopped parsley, to garnish

1 Grease a frying pan or a griddle with a little oil and slightly brown the aubergine rounds on both sides.

2 Preheat the oven to 200°C/Fan 180°C/ Gas 6. Put the onion, garlic and olive oil in a frying pan and sauté for 5 minutes until the onion has softened. Add the cinnamon, black pepper and mixed spices and stir for 2 minutes.

3 Place the chicken breasts in a baking dish. Spread the onion over the chicken pieces, then add the aubergine and lastly the tomatoes. Pour the diluted tomato purée over the top and sprinkle over the salt.

4 Bake in a preheated oven for 30–40 minutes until the chicken is cooked through.

5 Garnish with the parsley, then serve with plain basmati, or saffron rice (see page 233).

Okra with Lamb
Yakhnet Bameyeh

Okra (*bameyeh*) is one of the most popular vegetables throughout the Middle East. It is an acquired taste and is usually cooked with lamb or beef, or without meat as a vegetarian dish.

SERVES 4

PREPARATION TIME
15–20 minutes

COOKING TIME
50 minutes or
30 minutes for the
vegetarian version

COOK'S TIP
Some people like
extra lemon, so we
tend to serve this
with lemon wedges
on the side.

400g lamb or beef, cut into cubes
1 litre boiling water
1 large onion (about 250g), coarsely chopped
6 garlic cloves
30ml olive oil
1 tsp salt
½ tsp ground black pepper
1 tsp ground cinnamon
500g okra, top ends trimmed
3 tomatoes (about 250g), chopped
2 tbsp tomato purée
Juice of 1 lemon (about 30ml) or
  ½ tbsp pomegranate molasses
30g coriander, chopped, reserving
  a few leaves for the garnish

1 Boil the meat in the boiling water for 5 minutes. Turn the heat down to medium, cover the pan and simmer for 30–40 minutes.

2 Fry the onion and garlic in the olive oil over a medium heat for 5 minutes. Remove the meat from the stock and fry with the onion and garlic for another 5 minutes. Add the salt, pepper and cinnamon and stir for 1 minute.

3 Return the meat with the onion and garlic to the stock. Add the okra, tomatoes and tomato purée to the meat and stock and cook for a further 15 minutes.

4 Add the lemon juice or molasses and the coriander and cook for another 5 minutes.

5 Serve garnished with the reserved coriander leaves and plain basmati or Lebanese vermicelli rice (see page 239).

Herb and Chilli Fish Fillets

Samack Ma'a Couzbarah

This full-of-flavour dish is so simple and quick to make. You can have it on the table in less than half an hour.

SERVES 4

PREPARATION TIME
10 minutes, plus
marinating

COOKING TIME
15 minutes

COOK'S TIP
I prefer to heat the oil
and garlic together
instead of adding the
garlic to hot oil,
in which it may burn.

½ tsp salt
1 tsp ground cumin
800g skinless white fish fillets, skinned
20ml olive oil

FOR THE TOPPING
4 garlic cloves, finely chopped
20ml olive oil
50g coriander, chopped
1 red chilli, deseeded and sliced
2 lemon wedges, to serve
Salt

1 Rub the salt and cumin all over the fish and allow it to marinate for 10 minutes.

2 Heat the oil over a medium heat. Shallow fry the fish for 10 minutes, turning it during cooking to slightly brown on both sides. Set aside to keep warm.

3 For the topping, put the garlic and oil in a frying pan and fry for a few seconds (avoid browning). Just when you start to smell the garlic, add the coriander, chilli and salt to taste and stir together for 1 minute.

4 Plate the fish and spread the topping over.

5 Serve with lemon wedges and a salad of your choice.

Chicken with Rice and Nuts

Oozy

This is a special dish throughout the Middle East. It is always served at special occasions, such as weddings, either with chicken – as described here – or lamb, where a whole roasted lamb is placed on the rice and nuts. Despite this heritage, the recipe is simple enough to serve at any time.

SERVES 4

PREPARATION TIME
5 minutes

COOKING TIME
2 hours
.

1.5kg whole free-range organic chicken
1 tsp ground cinnamon
½ tsp mixed spices (see page 237)
½ tsp salt
½ tsp allspice

FOR THE RICE
500g long-grain rice, rinsed and soaked
100g split almonds, toasted
30g pine nuts, toasted
100g minced beef (optional)
1 tsp ground cinnamon
½ tsp ground black pepper
1 tsp mixed spices (see page 237)
1 tsp salt

1 Preheat the oven to 190ºC/Fan 170ºC/ Gas 5, rub the chicken with the cinnamon, mixed spices, salt and allspice, then place in a roasting tin and roast for about 90 minutes, making sure it's well cooked.

2 When the chicken is cooked, remove it from the oven and cover it with foil. Drain the rice from its soaking water.

3 Drain some of the chicken fat from the roasting tin and pour it into a saucepan. Fry the minced meat over a medium heat for 2–3 minutes until it becomes brown and crispy. Add the spices and turn for 1 minute. Add the drained rice and top with water until it's about 1cm above the rice level.

4 When most of the water has evaporated (about 5 minutes), turn the heat down to low, cover and simmer for about 15–20 minutes. The rice should be dry and fluffy.

5 Cut the chicken into small pieces. Turn the rice out onto a flat serving dish, place the chicken pieces over the rice and spread the nuts over the top.

6 Serve with natural yogurt and a salad. I love Arabian salad (see page 185) with this dish.

Lentils with Wholegrain Rice and Caramelised Onions
Mdardara

It might surprise you to see how you can make a tasty dish with only four ingredients. This is a very old-fashioned dish and is popular in all of Lebanon. It's now a trend to serve the old recipes, even in restaurants.

SERVES 4

PREPARATION TIME
10–15 minutes

COOKING TIME
50 minutes

150g brown or green lentils, rinsed
1 litre boiling water
100ml olive oil
2 very large onions (about 450g),
  halved and thinly sliced
300g wholegrain rice
1 tsp salt

1 Cook the lentils in the boiling water (no salt at this stage) for about 30 minutes over a medium heat. The lentils should be cooked but make sure they don't overcook. Drain and keep the water as stock.

2 Meanwhile, heat the oil in a large frying pan and fry the onions over a medium heat for 15 minutes until they become slightly brown. Remove two-thirds of the onions and set aside to add to the lentils. Continue to fry the remaining third of onions for roughly 5 more minutes until they are golden brown and crispy. Set aside on kitchen paper. When the lentils are ready and drained, stir through the first two-thirds of onion.

3 Put the rice in a saucepan and cover with lentil stock over the rice by 2cm. Add the salt, cover and cook over a low heat for 10 minutes until most of the stock has evaporated.

4 Add the lentil-and-onion mixture to the rice and fold with a wooden spoon, cover and simmer for another 10 minutes until all the moisture has gone.

5 Turn the rice mixture out onto a serving dish and top with the crispy onions.

6 Serve hot or cold with condiments, such as natural yogurt and minty tomato salad.

Baked Courgette Slices with Minced Beef
Ablama

This dish is usually made with whole baby courgettes, hollowed out and stuffed with a minced meat mixture. For a short cut, I slice the courgettes – simpler, but the flavour is just as good.

SERVES 4

PREPARATION TIME
15 minutes

COOKING TIME
45 minutes

1kg courgettes, washed, trimmed and sliced into 2cm-thick rounds
50ml olive oil
15g pine nuts
2 onions (about 350g), chopped
400g lean minced beef
1 tsp salt
½ tsp ground black pepper
1 tsp ground cinnamon
100g tomato purée diluted in ½ litre hot water

1 Preheat the oven to 200ºC/Fan 180ºC/ Gas 6. Coat the courgette slices with 20ml of the oil, place them on a baking tray and bake for 15 minutes until brown.

2 While the courgettes are in the oven, prepare the filling. Heat the remaining oil in a frying pan over a medium heat. Add the pine nuts, cook for 2–3 minutes until browned, then set them aside on kitchen paper.

3 Place the onions in the oil in the pan and fry until brown. Add the mince and fry for a further 5 minutes to brown the meat. Then add half the pine nuts, the salt, pepper and cinnamon, stirring for a few seconds.

4 When the courgettes are ready, remove the baking tray from the oven and line an ovenproof dish with half the courgettes, spread the mince over the top then cover with the remaining courgettes, pour over the diluted tomato purée and place the dish in the oven to bake for 30 minutes until the sauce has thickened.

5 Serve on a bed of plain or vermicelli rice (see page 239), sprinkled with the remaining pine nuts.

Chicken with Freekeh (Green Wheat)

Djaj Ma Freekeh

In some parts of Lebanon, people don't know what *freekeh* is and in other parts it is used frequently instead of rice. *Freekeh* has been a main ingredient in the Middle East for centuries. It is tasty and a real super food with a high protein and fibre content.

SERVES 4

PREPARATION TIME
10 minutes

COOKING TIME
About 75 minutes

1.5kg whole free-range, organic chicken
3 garlic cloves
1 tsp ground cinnamon
½ tsp ground black pepper
½ tsp mixed spices or allspice (see page 237)
1 tsp salt
2 bay leaves
20ml olive oil
2 medium onions (about 300g), chopped
400g freekeh, rinsed and soaked for 20 minutes
30g toasted almonds
20g toasted pine nuts

1 Skin the chicken, cut it into quarters and place it in a saucepan. Just cover it with hot water. Add the garlic, cinnamon, pepper, mixed spices or allspice, salt and bay leaves. Cook for 45 minutes over a medium heat, until the chicken is very tender and the water reduced.

2 Add the oil and onions to a large frying pan and fry over a medium heat for a 2–3 minutes until the onions are slightly browned. Add the *freekeh*, then add the chicken stock to 2cm above the *freekeh*.

3 Boil for 5 minutes, then reduce the heat to low then simmer for another 15–20 minutes, stirring once or twice until all the water has evaporated.

4 While the *freekeh* is cooking, remove the chicken from the bones and tear it into small pieces.

5 Turn the *freekeh* out onto a serving dish, place the chicken pieces over the top, then sprinkle the almonds and pine nuts over the top.

6 Serve with plain yogurt and/or any salad of your choice (see the salads chapter).

Lemony Cauliflower and Beef Stew
Yakhnet Karnabeet

Stews are a very popular, everyday family food in Lebanon, always served with rice and easy to prepare. Many think of cauliflower as a boring vegetable, but you will enjoy it cooked this way.

SERVES 4

PREPARATION TIME
10 minutes

COOKING TIME
40 minutes

1kg cauliflower florets (1 large cauliflower head)
50ml olive oil
2 medium onions (about 300g), chopped
500g braising beef, cut into small cubes
4 garlic cloves, crushed
1 tsp ground cinnamon
500ml hot water
Juice of 2 large lemons (about 70ml)
40g coriander, chopped
1 tsp salt

1 Preheat the oven to 200°C/Fan 180°C/Gas 6. Rinse the cauliflower, drain, drizzle with 20ml of the oil, spread over a baking tray and roast for 35 minutes until brown.

2 While the cauliflower is in the oven, fry the onions for 5–10 minutes in a large pan in the remaining oil over a medium heat until slightly brown.

3 Add the beef and fry it with the onions for 5 minutes, then add the garlic and cinnamon and stir for 1 minute. Add the hot water, cover and simmer over a medium to low heat for 30 minutes until the meat is really tender.

4 Add the roasted florets, the lemon juice, 30g of the coriander and the salt to the pan and cook for another 10 minutes. Remove from the heat and serve garnished with the remaining coriander and plain or Lebanese vermicelli rice (see page 239).

Upside-down Vegetable and Spiced Rice Pot
Makloubeh

With the presence of Palestinians in Lebanon over the last 70 years, Palestinian dishes like this one have integrated into Lebanese cuisine. It is mostly made with lamb and aubergines or cauliflower and chicken. Here is a vegetable version that you can serve as a vegetarian dish, or with roasted chicken served on the side.

SERVES 6

PREPARATION TIME
20 minutes

COOKING TIME
1 hour and
45 minutes

COOK'S TIP
To make the saffron water, soak the saffron strands in 2 tablespoons of water before using – this boosts the colour and flavour.

1.5 kg free-range, organic chicken
1½ tsp salt, plus extra for sprinkling
350g squash or pumpkin, peeled and deseeded and cut into chunks
1 large aubergine (about 300g), cut into 8 pieces
500g cauliflower florets
150g carrots, halved lengthways
2 red peppers (about 250g), deseeded and quartered
60ml olive oil
2 large onions (about 500g), sliced
300g basmati rice, soaked for 30 minutes
1 tsp ground cinnamon
1 tsp allspice
½ tsp ground nutmeg
2 tbsp saffron water (see cook's tip) (optional)
40g almonds, toasted
20g pine nuts, toasted
1 tbsp chopped parsley, to garnish

1 Preheat the oven to 180°C/Fan 160°C/Gas 4. Sprinkle the chicken with a little salt, place in a roasting tray and roast for 1 hour 45 minutes, until cooked through.

2 Mix all the vegetables except the onions with ½ tsp salt and 20ml of the oil. Spread the vegetables over a baking tray and roast in the oven for 30 minutes with the chicken, until fairly brown. Remove from the oven and set aside.

3 While the chicken and vegetables are roasting, put the remaining oil and the onions in a frying pan and fry over a medium heat for about 15 minutes until they are soft and lightly browned. Set aside.

4 When the vegetables are ready, line the bottom of a large saucepan with them.

5 Drain the rice and mix with the sautéed onions, all the spices and 1 teaspoon of salt, then spread the mixture evenly over the vegetables. Add water to cover the rice by 1cm and add the saffron water, if using.

6 Place the pan over a medium heat. When the liquid starts to boil leave it until most of the liquid is absorbed, then turn the heat to low, cover and simmer for 35 minutes. Test the rice. If it's still not cooked enough, add a few tablespoons of water and cook for another 5 minutes or so.

7 Remove from the heat and leave to rest for 5 minutes. Place a round serving plate over the pot and carefully turn it upside down and remove the pan.

8 Spread the nuts over the top and garnish with a little chopped parsley.

9 When the chicken is ready, cut the chicken into pieces and serve alongside the rice along with natural yogurt – they go so well together.

Fish with Zaatar and Sumac

Samack Bzaatar Wsumac

The first time I had this dish it was cooked by a friend and, honestly, I was a bit hesitant. Then I tried it and realised the combination of flavours work so deliciously well. I've made it several times since.

SERVES 4

PREPARATION TIME
10 minutes

COOKING TIME
30 minutes

2 lemons, juice of 1 (about 30ml), and the second sliced
1.5kg grey or red snapper, gutted and rinsed
1 green pepper (about 100g), deseeded and diced
1 red pepper (about 100g), deseeded and diced
6 cloves of garlic (about 100g), crushed
3 tsp zaatar
2 tsp ground coriander
4 tsp sumac
30ml olive oil
1 tsp salt

1 Preheat the oven to 220ºC/Fan 200ºC/ Gas 7. Line the inside of the fish with the lemon slices. Wrap the fish in foil and bake in the oven for 20 minutes.

2 Meanwhile, prepare a paste by mixing all the remaining ingredients together.

3 When the fish is ready, take out of the oven and open out the 2 sides to cool a little before handling.

4 Remove all the bones and the skin and place all the fish pieces on a baking tray or an ovenproof dish and top with the paste mixture. Return to the oven for 10 minutes.

5 Serve hot or cold with Lebanese-style potato salad (see page 193) and any green salad of your choice.

Borlotti Bean Mjadra

Mjadara Fasoulia

All Lebanese are familiar with lentil *mjadra*, but only the Christians in Lebanon know this dish, which is just as delicious. Christians in Lebanon take the six weeks of Lent very seriously and eat only plant food for the whole of Lent. As a result many have become creative with food and created some amazing dishes.

SERVES 4

PREPARATION TIME
5–10 minutes

COOKING TIME
40 minutes, or
1½ hours, if using
dried beans

400g cooked or 200g dried borlotti beans
50ml olive oil
1 large onion (about 200g), chopped
3 garlic cloves, crushed
1 tsp salt
40g coriander, chopped

1 If using dried beans, soak the beans for 6 hours or overnight. Drain, place the beans in a saucepan, add water and bring to the boil, then simmer over a low heat for about 50 minutes, until the beans are tender in the middle. Drain.

2 Heat 30ml of the oil in a saucepan and fry the onion over a medium heat for about 10 minutes until browned. Add the garlic and stir with the onion for 1 minute.

3 Add the drained beans to the onion mixture, then add the salt and enough boiling water to just cover the beans. Cover and simmer over a low heat for 30 minutes until the moisture has evaporated.

4 Crush the beans with a fork so they are roughly mashed and add the remaining olive oil. (Most people use a blender, but I prefer the coarse texture.)

5 Serve hot or cold with any salad and flatbread.

Chicken Coated with Pistachios
Djaj B Fustok

We often have chicken dishes served with toasted nuts and rice. Here I tried to exclude the rice to have a healthier and a lower calorie meal of chicken with pistachios. It's amazingly simple and tasty.

SERVES 4

PREPARATION TIME
About 10 minutes

COOKING TIME
30 minutes

3 garlic cloves, crushed
Juice of 1 lemon (about 30ml)
40ml olive oil
1 tsp ginger root, grated
¼ tsp ground white pepper
4 large skinless chicken breasts (about 100g each)
½ tsp salt
120g pistachios, crushed

1 In a large bowl, mix the crushed garlic with the lemon juice, oil, ginger and pepper to make a marinade.

2 Slash the chicken breasts a few times, add them to the marinade and turn to coat. Cover and marinate for 2–3 hours in the fridge.

3 Preheat the oven to 200ºC/Fan 180ºC/ Gas 6. Now add the salt just before cooking. Coat the chicken breasts on both sides by rolling in the crushed pistachios.

4 Place the chicken on a baking tray and bake for 25–30 minutes in the oven.

5 Remove the chicken from the oven and cover with foil for a few minutes before serving to retain the moisture.

6 Serve with spinach and soya bean salad (see page 195) or another salad or vegetable side dish of your choice. I frequently choose roasted cauliflower.

Kafta Meatballs in Tomato Sauce
Dawood Basha

Kafta is minced lamb or beef, combined with chopped parsley, onions and a few spices. It is cooked in a variety of dishes and is very popular throughout the Middle East.

SERVES 4

PREPARATION TIME
15–20 minutes

COOKING TIME
45 minutes

FOR THE KAFTA
500g minced lamb
1 medium onion (about 150g), grated or
finely chopped
1 tsp ground cinnamon
1 tsp salt
½ tsp allspice
½ tsp ground black pepper
70g parsley, chopped

FOR THE SAUCE
25g olive oil
1 large onion (about 200g), diced
350g tomatoes, chopped
300g carrots, peeled and sliced
50g tomato purée diluted with 400ml
warm water
1 tsp salt

1 Reserving a little of the parsley, combine all the *kafta* ingredients together and mix well. Roll into small balls about 4cm in diameter. This will make about 15 balls. Set aside.

2 Prepare the sauce by heating the oil and onion in a saucepan over a medium heat. Fry for a few minutes or until the onion is golden brown.

3 Add the tomatoes, carrots, diluted tomato purée and salt.

4 When the sauce boils, add the meatballs, making sure they are well coated in the sauce. Cook for 30 minutes until the sauce is thickened.

5 Serve on a bed of plain or vermicelli rice (see page 239) and sprinkle with the reserved parsley.

Lamb and Aubergine Casserole

Ghanam Ma Batingane

As I mentioned before, the Lebanese eat a little meat when it's included in some dishes. This is a lovely, delicious combination of lamb and aubergines.

SERVES 4–6

PREPARATION TIME
10 minutes

COOKING TIME
About 4 hours

1.5kg leg or shoulder of lamb on the bone
30ml olive oil
2 large onions (about 450g), coarsely chopped
6 garlic cloves
1 tsp ground cinnamon
½ tsp ground black pepper
1 tsp allspice
1½ tsp salt
1 tin (400g) good-quality chopped tomatoes
2 large aubergines (about 550g), cut into cubes
Small amount of parsley, chopped

1 Preheat the oven to 180°C/Fan 160°C/Gas 4. Heat the oil in a casserole dish over a medium heat. Add the meat and slightly brown it all over to seal it.

2 Add the onions and garlic to the pan and fry with the lamb over a low heat for 5 minutes. Add the cinnamon, pepper, allspice and salt and stir with the onions for 2 minutes.

3 Add the chopped tomatoes and 300ml of water. Cover the casserole and place in the oven to slow cook for about 3 hours.

4 Add the aubergines and turn to coat them in the sauce. Return the dish to the oven and cook for another 40 minutes until the aubergines are well cooked and the meat is falling off the bone.

5 Serve with plain basmati rice and garnish with a little parsley.

Sumac Chicken Wraps
Musakhan

Don't skip the page when you see the amount of onion in this dish. It is delicious and really worth trying. *Musakhan* is a traditional Palestinian dish added to Lebanese cuisine owing to the presence of Palestinians in Lebanon over the last seventy years.

SERVES 4

PREPARATION TIME
30 minutes

COOKING TIME
1 hour and
35 minutes

COOK'S TIP
If you can't find Lebanese bread, you can use tortilla wraps or pitta bread and fill them as pockets.

1.5kg free-range, organic chicken
80ml olive oil
4 large onions (about 800g), chopped
30g sumac
1 tsp salt
4 Lebanese (see page 234) or other flatbread

1 Preheat oven to 200ºC/Fan 180ºC/Gas 6. Put the chicken in a roasting tin and roast for 1½ hours, until the chicken is cooked through and the skin is crispy brown.

2 Meanwhile reserve 20ml of the oil for brushing later and heat the remaining 60ml in a large frying pan. Sauté the onions for 30 minutes over a medium heat until they begin to turn a little brown. Add the sumac and salt then mix well.

3 When the chicken is ready, remove it from the oven and leave to cool down enough to handle. (Leave the oven on.)

4 Remove the flesh from the bones, break it into small pieces and mix (including the crispy skin) with the onions and sumac.

5 Split each loaf in half. Divide the sumac chicken equally between the flatbread halves, then fold over the end and sides and roll to create a wrap.

6 Lightly grease a baking tray with a little of the reserved oil. Place the wraps on the tray close together and brush the surface of each wrap with the remaining oil.

7 Place the wraps in the oven for 5 minutes, so the surface is slightly coloured and crispy.

8 Serve hot or cold.

Borlotti Beans with Tomatoes and Garlic
Fasoulia Bzeit

As I mentioned, pulses are very popular and we just love to use them to create meat-free dishes. This dish can be made with any beans you like, but I have used borlotti.

SERVES 4

PREPARATION TIME
10 minutes

COOKING TIME
30 minutes, plus
1 hour if using dried
beans

750g cooked or 375g dried borlotti beans
1 large onion (about 250g), chopped
30ml olive oil
4 garlic cloves, crushed
1 heaped tsp ground cumin
½ tsp ground black pepper
400g tomatoes, chopped
50g tomato purée diluted with 50ml water
1 tsp salt
45g coriander, chopped

1 If using dried beans, soak them overnight, then boil them for about 1 hour until the beans are very tender in the middle (don't add salt at this stage otherwise the beans will remain hard). Drain.

2 Place the onion and oil together in a pan and fry for 5–10 minutes over a medium heat until the onion is golden brown.

3 Add the garlic and stir for 1 minute, then add the cumin and pepper and stir for another 1 minute.

4 Add the chopped tomatoes, diluted tomato purée, and salt. Cover the pan and simmer for 5 minutes. Add the beans and continue to cook for 15 minutes. Add the coriander (reserving a little for the garnish) and cook for another 5 minutes, until the sauce is thick and rich.

5 Transfer to a serving bowl, garnish with the remaining coriander and serve with rice or bread.

Fish and Bulgur Wheat Pie

Kebbeh Samack

Kebbeh is the Lebanese national dish and is mostly made with beef. Fish *kebbeh* is less common and more specialised. Sometimes *kebbeh* is made with mashed pumpkin as a vegetarian option.

SERVES 4–6

PREPARATION TIME
25 minutes (approx)

COOKING TIME
1 hour

FOR THE KEBBEH
200g fine bulgur wheat (burghul),
  rinsed and drained
500g skinless white fish fillets
1 large onion (about 150g), grated
1 tsp ground turmeric
1 tsp ground cinnamon
1 tsp allspice
½ tsp ground black pepper
2 tsp ground cumin
2 tsp ground coriander
1 tsp salt
Grated rind of 1 lemon
30g coriander leaves, chopped

FOR THE FILLING
4 large onions (about 900g), halved and sliced
60ml olive oil, plus extra for greasing
½ tsp white pepper
1 tsp turmeric
20g pine nuts, toasted
25g split almonds
Pinch of saffron (optional)
Salt

1 Rinse the bulgur wheat, drain all the water and leave aside to absorb the moisture until soft.

2 Meanwhile, combine the fish and onion in a blender and add the fish mixture to the bulgur wheat with all the remaining *kebbeh* ingredients. Mix well as if you are kneading dough, then set aside while you prepare the filling.

3 Place the onions and 30ml of the oil in a large frying pan. Sauté the onion over a medium heat for 10 minutes, then add salt, the pepper, turmeric and pine nuts and stir for another 5 minutes.

4 Preheat the oven to 200°C/Fan 180°C/ Gas 6. Grease the bottom and sides of a 30cm baking tray.

5 Divide the *kebbeh* in half. Evenly and smoothly spread 1 half of the *kebbeh* over the base of the tray, then spread the filling over the top. Taking a handful of *kebbeh*, flatten it between your palms and place the flattened *kebbeh* over the filling. Repeat until all the filing is covered with the remaining *kebbeh*. Smooth the surface with your hands.

6 With a knife, cut through only the first layer of the *kebbeh*, making squares or diamond-shape pieces.

7 Place the almonds over the top, drizzle with the remaining oil, and sprinkle over the saffron strands, if using, then bake in the oven for 50 minutes until the top is browned.

8 Remove the tray from the oven and rest the *kebbeh* for 10 minutes before serving (resting makes it easier to cut into slices).

9 Serve warm with a salad of your choice.

Fish and Tomato Stew
Yakhnet Samack

Meat or vegetable stews are the most common everyday food cooked for the family. It's uncommon to use fish, but it's getting more and more popular.

SERVES 4

PREPARATION TIME
10 minutes

COOKING TIME
35 minutes

700g chunky mild skinless white fish fillets
  (such as cod or monkfish)
40ml olive oil
2 onions (about 250g), chopped
3–4 garlic cloves, sliced
500g ripe vine tomatoes, chopped
Ground black pepper
30g parsley, chopped
1 lemon, cut into wedges, to serve
Salt

1 Cut the fish into large cubes and sprinkle with a little salt.

2 Heat the oil in a casserole and fry the onions and garlic for 5 minutes over a medium heat until golden brown.

3 Add the tomatoes, pepper and salt. Cover the pan and simmer over a low heat for 20 minutes.

4 Reserving a little chopped parsley for the garnish, mix the parsley with the tomato mixture.

5 Add the fish pieces to the casserole and turn gently to coat with the sauce. Simmer for another 10 minutes. Garnish with the reserved chopped parsley.

6 Serve with cumin (see page 240) or saffron rice (see page 230) and lemon wedges on the side.

Mediterranean Vegetables and Lamb Bake
Saneyet Khoudra

Packed with nutrients, this dish is tasty and very easy to prepare.
You can make it with lamb or beef, or leave the meat out altogether.
Once the chopping and slicing is done, there is no effort needed to
cook this dish whatsoever.

SERVES 4 OR MORE

PREPARATION TIME
20 minutes

COOKING TIME
70 minutes

COOK'S TIP
This recipe works well
without the meat for
a vegetarian version.

400g minced lamb or beef
2 large onions (about 400g), sliced
1 tsp ground cinnamon
1 tsp allspice
½ tsp ground black pepper
300g courgettes, sliced
400g potatoes, cut into cubes
1 large aubergine (about 300g), cut into cubes
200g French beans, trimmed and halved
1 large red pepper (about 250g), deseeded and
    cut into strips
300g carrots, sliced
150g tomatoes, sliced
1 tsp salt
100g tomato purée
300ml warm water

1 Preheat the oven to 200ºC/Fan 180ºC/
Gas 6. In a large, deep baking tray, mix the
meat, onions, cinnamon, allspice and pepper
together with your hands.

2 Add the remaining vegetables, except the
tomatoes, turning and mixing everything
together to fully combine.

3 In a small jug mix together the salt and
tomato purée. Add 300ml of warm water,
stir, then add to the vegetables. Turn to coat
all the ingredients with the tomato sauce.

4 Bake in the oven for 50 minutes, then take
the tray out of the oven, turn vegetables once
with a wooden spoon and place the sliced
tomatoes over the top. Return the tray to the
oven and bake for another 20 minutes until
the surface is crispy and looking slightly
burnt and most of the liquid is absorbed.

5 Serve with flatbread and chilli sauce
(see page 231), if you wish.

Lentils with Spinach

Adas wa Sabanekh

This super-food dish will accommodate vegetarians, vegans, fish-eaters and meat-eaters. It is served on its own or with feta cheese crumbled over the top and any grilled fish, meat or chicken.

SERVES 4

PREPARATION TIME
15 minutes

COOKING TIME
50 minutes

300g green lentils, rinsed
2 onions (about 250g), chopped
2–3 garlic cloves, chopped
40ml olive oil, plus 1 tbsp for the lentils
500g fresh or frozen spinach
1 tsp salt
½ tsp ground black pepper
1 lemon, cut into wedges, to serve

1 Cook the lentils in boiling water in a covered pan over a low heat, for about 50 minutes until most of the water has evaporated and the lentils are well cooked.

2 While the lentils are cooking, put the onions, garlic and oil in a frying pan and sauté the onions and garlic over a low heat for about 15 minutes. Add the spinach leaves, half the salt and the pepper and cook for 10–15 minutes until the spinach is cooked and most of the moisture is evaporated.

3 When the lentils are cooked, add the remaining ½ a teaspoon of salt, and the 1 tablespoon of oil and mix well.

4 Serve the lentils with the sautéed onions and the spinach over the top with bread or any grilled fish or meat of your choice, or simply crumble feta cheese over the top. Serve the lemon wedges on the side.

Marinated Chicken Cubes
Djaj Tawouk

This fabulous way of serving chicken is one of our national dishes. It can be served as a meal on its own, as part of a mixed grill or as a fast-food wrap combined with salad and pickles.

SERVES 4

PREPARATION TIME
10 minutes, plus
marinating

COOKING TIME
20 minutes

1kg skinless chicken breasts (4 large breasts), each cut into 6 cubes
1 each of red, yellow and green peppers (about 600g in total), deseeded and cut into chunks
350g courgettes, cut into 3cm thick slices
4 small onions (about 250g), quartered
30ml olive oil
Salt

FOR THE MARINADE
4–5 garlic cloves, crushed
3 tbsp natural yogurt
2 tbsp mayonnaise
2 tbsp olive oil
Juice of 1 lemon (about 30ml)
½ tsp chilli powder (optional)
1 tsp paprika
1 tsp salt

1 Place all the marinade ingredients in a bowl, stir to combine, then and add the chicken pieces, turning them over a few times until they are well coated in the marinade. Cover and keep in the fridge for at least 4 hours. The longer the better.

2 When you are ready to cook, rub the vegetables with the 30ml of olive oil and sprinkle with a little salt. Thread the vegetables onto skewers. On separate skewers, thread on the marinated chicken pieces. (If using wooden skewers, soak them in water before using.)

3 Either grill or barbecue the skewers for about 20 minutes until the meat is cooked through and the vegetables are soft and charred at the edges. Test a piece of chicken by cutting through the middle to make sure it's well cooked and no pink remains, and make sure you don't overcook it either, as it will be dry.

4 Serve with Lebanese or pitta bread, a salad of your choice and garlic sauce (see page 238).

Aleppo-style Kebab
Kebab Halaby

This kebab recipe originated in Aleppo, in Syria, and became popular throughout the Middle East. It is full of delicious flavours, yet so simple barbecued or grilled.

SERVES 4

PREPARATION TIME
15 minutes

COOKING TIME
10 minutes

70g pistachios
500g minced lamb
1 chilli, finely chopped (optional)
¼ tsp ground chilli powder, to taste
1 tsp ground ginger
1 tsp Lebanese mixed spices (see page 237)
¼ tsp ground black pepper
½ tsp salt or more, to season

1 First prepare the pistachios. Roughly crush 30g and coarsely chop the remainder to resemble coarse breadcrumbs.

2 Place the lamb in a mixing bowl, add the chilli (if using), all the spices, the pepper, salt and roughly crushed pistachios. Mix thoroughly with your hands and allow the meat to rest for 10 minutes.

3 Divide the meat into about 8–10 balls, each about the size of a small egg. Roll each ball between your palms until it resembles a sausage and coat each one with chopped pistachios. Push skewers through and squeeze the sausages tight so they don't fall off the skewers while cooking. (If using wooden skewers soak them in water first before using.)

4 Grill or barbecue the kebabs for 10 minutes on a high heat, turning them once during cooking to ensure both sides are evenly cooked.

5 Serve with pitta bread and *freekeh* (green wheat) salad (see page 89) or any salad of your choice. They are also delicious served with hummus for dipping.

Lentils and Bulgur Wheat
Mjadara Ma'a Burghul

With its few ingredients, mjadara is one of the most popular dishes in Lebanon – and so economical to make. Mjadara is always served with different salads that complement its mild flavour. It is more common to make it with rice than bulgur wheat, but this is an even healthier option.

SERVES 4

PREPARATION TIME
10 minutes

COOKING TIME
About 1 hour and 20 minutes

1.5 litres boiling water
250g green lentils
2 medium–large onions (about 300g), chopped
50ml olive oil
150g coarse bulgur wheat (burghul)
1 heaped tsp salt

1 Add the boiling water to the lentils and boil for 2–3 minutes, then cover the saucepan, turn the heat down to low and simmer for about 45 minutes, depending on the type of lentils, until they're really soft.

2 Meanwhile, fry the onions with 30ml of the oil over a medium heat for about 10 minutes until the onions are brown. When the lentils are ready, add the onions to the lentils and cook for another 10 minutes.

3 Rinse and drain the bulgur wheat, and add to the lentils and onions with the salt. Keep simmering and stirring occasionally for 20–25 minutes until most of the moisture has evaporated, making sure the mjadara is not too dry. Add a little more water if necessary.

4 Remove the mjadara from the heat, then add the remaining 20ml of oil with a quick stir.

5 Serve warm or cold with any salad or natural yogurt. (See salads chapter.)

Bulgur Wheat and Beef-filled Balls in Yogurt
Kebbeh Labaneyeh

This is not an everyday dish, just because it requires more time and effort to prepare. Cooking with yogurt is so popular and this is one of the favourite traditional dishes that are cooked in yogurt.

SERVES 4–6

PREPARATION TIME
45 minutes

COOKING TIME
50 minutes

FOR THE KEBBEH
200g fine bulgur wheat (burghul),
  rinsed and drained
1 onion (about 130g), grated
250g ground beef
1 tsp ground cumin
½ tsp salt
1 tsp marjoram
½ tsp ground black pepper

FOR THE FILLING
2 onions (about 200g), diced
30ml olive oil
200g minced beef
½ tsp salt
½ tsp ground black pepper
1 tsp ground cinnamon
10g pine nuts, toasted

FOR THE SAUCE
2 tsp cornflour, mixed with 200ml water
½ tsp salt
2 litres natural yogurt
3 garlic cloves, crushed
2 tsp dried mint
30ml olive oil
½ tsp sumac (optional)

1 Put all the kebbeh ingredients in a bowl, mix thoroughly until it looks and feels like a dough. You may need to add a little more water as the burghul swells. Set aside.

2 Put the onions and oil in a frying pan and fry for 10 minutes over a medium heat until the onion is almost browned. Add the minced beef and fry for a further 5 minutes.

Add the salt, pepper, cinnamon and pine nuts. Stir for 1 minute. Set aside.

3 To make the sauce, add the cornflour mixture and salt to the yogurt and stir well until you can't see any lumps. (Cornflour stops the yogurt from curdling.) Start cooking the yogurt in a pan over a medium heat, stirring all the time, for about 10 minutes, or until the yogurt begins to boil. Turn the heat down and allow the yogurt to simmer gently for 10–15 minutes, stirring occasionally.

4 Take a piece of kebbeh dough and roll it between the palms of your hands to make a golf ball-sized ball.

5 Make a hollow shell as thin as possible from your ball of dough. Fill the hole with the filling and seal the open end, making sure there are no cracks in the dough. If it sticks to your hands, just dampen your hands with water. Repeat with the remaining dough and filling. Once you have filled all the balls (about 10 in total), make each one into a longer shape, like a mini rugby ball.

6 Add the kebbeh balls into the simmering yogurt, keeping them separated to avoid sticking, and cook for 15 minutes.

7 In a separate frying pan, fry the garlic and mint in the oil for 1 minute and add to the surface of the yogurt. Cook for 2–3 minutes.

8 Serve this dish on its own, just as it comes, or add a sprinkle of sumac.

Aubergine with Chickpeas
Maghmoura

This dish is frequently cooked in the countryside where people often had meat-free days many years ago when meat was not always available and therefore substituted with pulses. Like many old-fashioned foods, it has become popular everywhere and is served in restaurants with the starters spread (maza), but in small portions.

SERVES 4

PREPARATION TIME
10 minutes

COOKING TIME
30 minutes

2 medium onions (about 300g), sliced
6–7 garlic cloves, whole
60ml olive oil
2 large aubergines (about 600g), cut into strips
600g tomatoes, cut in half and sliced
½ tsp ground black pepper
1 tsp salt
400g cooked chickpeas (see page 39)

1 Mix the onions and garlic with 30ml of the oil and fry in a frying pan over a medium heat for 5 minutes until soft and slightly browned.

2 Add the aubergine slices and fry with the onions and garlic for a further 5–10 minutes until softened and brown in places.

3 Add the sliced tomatoes, pepper and salt. Turn the heat down to low and simmer for 10 minutes.

4 Add the chickpeas, turning them a little with a wooden spoon. Try to avoid squashing the aubergines.

5 Cover and simmer for another 10 minutes until the juice has thickened.

6 Remove from the heat and drizzle with the remaining oil.

7 This dish is usually served cold with bread or hot with plain rice.

Fish with Herbs and Chilli
Samakeh Harrah

This traditional northern dish is full of flavour and goodness and is simple to make. You can use either individual small fish or one large one.

SERVES 4

PREPARATION TIME
10 minutes

COOKING TIME
35 minutes

1kg snapper or sea bass
6 garlic cloves, chopped
80g coriander
60g parsley
1 medium red pepper (about 150g)
1 red chilli, seeded
30ml olive oil
1 tsp salt
Tahini sauce (see page 241)

1 Gut and scale the fish then cut across it from just below the head towards the tail. (You can ask your fishmonger to prepare it if you prefer.)

2 Preheat the oven to 200ºC/Fan 180ºC/ Gas 6. Put the garlic, herbs, pepper, chilli and oil in an electric blender and blend until you have a rough purée.

3 Line a baking tray with a sheet of baking parchment, place the fish on top, then fill the inside of the fish with one third of the herb mixture. Spread the remaining mixture over the fish.

4 Bake in the oven for 30 minutes until the fish is cooked but still moist.

5 Take the fish out of the oven, pour the tahini sauce over it then return it to the oven and bake for another 5 minutes.

6 Serve with Lebanese-style potato salad (see page 193), a vegetable side dish and lemon wedges.

Bean Stew
Yakhnet Fasoulia

This stew is one of our favourite Lebanese stews, always appreciated by the whole family, especially the children. You can use any kind of beans, including butter beans, and it's perfectly okay to use tinned beans as long as you drain the water and rinse them well.

SERVES 4

PREPARATION TIME
10 minutes, plus
soaking if using
dried beans

COOKING TIME
50 minutes, plus
45 minutes, if using
dried beans

COOK'S TIP
Without the meat,
this recipe is suitable
for vegetarians and
vegans.

400g dried (800g cooked) beans
35ml olive oil
2 onions (about 280g), chopped
400g lamb or beef, cut into small cubes
5–6 garlic cloves, crushed
1 heaped tsp ground cinnamon,
   plus extra to garnish
½ tsp ground black pepper
90g tomato purée, diluted in 400ml water
30g coriander leaves, chopped, reserving a
   few whole leaves for the garnish
1 tsp salt

1 If using dried beans, soak them overnight so they cook more quickly. Drain and cook them in fresh water for about 45 minutes depending on the type. When tender in the middle, drain well and set aside.

2 Meanwhile, fry the oil and onions in a pan over a medium heat for about 5 minutes until slightly brown.

3 Add the meat and fry for another 5 minutes to brown the meat. Then add the garlic, cinnamon and pepper and stir for a 2–3 more minutes. Add the diluted tomato purée, cover the pan and simmer for 20 minutes until the meat is tender.

4 Add the beans to the meat sauce and cook for another 15 minutes until the sauce has thickened.

5 Finally, add the chopped coriander and the salt and cook for a further 5 minutes.

6 Garnish with the reserved coriander leaves and serve with plain basmati rice, sprinkled with a little cinnamon over the top, if you like.

Zesty Lemon and Garlic Chicken
Djaj Biltoom Welhamod

Chicken and lemon is always a lovely combination. Some people say they like chicken only when it doesn't taste of chicken. Funnily enough I know what they mean. This chicken tastes very zesty, tasty and is simple to prepare.

SERVES 4

PREPARATION TIME
15 minutes

COOKING TIME
35–40 minutes

1 Preheat the oven to 200°C/Fan 180°C/ Gas 6. Place the chicken pieces, potatoes and lemon pieces in a roasting tin or an oven dish.

2 Sprinkle over the coriander and mix through.

3 Combine the oil, lemon juice, garlic, paprika, pepper, salt and 500ml of water together in a small jug, then pour the mixture all over the chicken.

4 Bake for 35–40 minutes. The juice should have reduced and the chicken should be cooked through. The potatoes should be partly browned.

5 Remove the dish from the oven and garnish with the reserved coriander leaves.

6 Serve with salad. Some people like to serve it with vermicelli rice.

1.5kg chicken, cut into serving portions
800g potatoes, cut into cubes and washed or peeled
4 lemons, juice of 2 (about 50ml) and 2 cut into 8 pieces
30g coriander, chopped, reserving a few whole leaves for the garnish
50ml olive oil
5–6 garlic cloves, crushed
1 tsp paprika
½ tsp ground white pepper
1 tsp salt

Green and White Beans with Tomato and Garlic
Loubeyeh Ma'a Fasoulia

This dish is usually cooked just with green beans as it's delicious with plump beans inside the pod – but they are not frequently available. I add white beans for the extra protein so it can be served as a main dish.

SERVES 4

PREPARATION TIME
20 minutes

COOKING TIME
50 minutes,
plus 45 minutes,
if using dried beans

600g green beans
300g cooked or 150g dried white beans
  (fasoulia)
40ml olive oil
2 onions (about 250g), chopped
60g garlic (2 small or 1 large bulb), peeled and
  used as whole cloves
500g tomatoes, chopped
1 tsp salt

1 Trim the beans and break them into about 4cm-long pieces.

2 If using dried beans, cook them according to the instruction on page 173.

3 Heat the oil in a saucepan, add the onions and fry until brown. Add the garlic cloves and continue frying for another 2–3 minutes.

4 Add the green beans and sauté them for 10 minutes to soften them.

5 Add the tomatoes, prepared white beans and the salt. Cover the pan and cook over a low heat for 30 minutes until the beans are very tender.

6 Serve with rice or simply flatbread.

Spinach with Minced Beef and Pine Nuts
Sabanekh Blahmeh

This is a very popular dish, even among children and those less enthusiastic about eating spinach. This is frequently repeated in my children's households as it is quick and simple to make and their kids love it. You can use either fresh or frozen spinach. If using frozen spinach, allow it to thaw and squeeze the water out, otherwise it may end up with too much liquid as this dish has no thickening ingredient.

SERVES 4

PREPARATION TIME
15 minutes

COOKING TIME
About 40 minutes

1kg fresh or frozen spinach, roughly chopped
   if fresh
2 onions (about 300g), chopped
40ml olive oil
400g minced beef
1 tsp salt
1 heaped tsp ground cinnamon
½ tsp ground black pepper
300ml boiling water
Juice of 1–2 lemons (about 50ml), plus 1 lemon
   cut into slices, to serve
20g pine nuts, toasted

1 If using fresh spinach, rinse the leaves, then place them in a colander to drain.

2 Fry the onions in a pan in the oil over a medium heat for about 5 minutes until golden brown. Add the minced beef and continue frying for 10 minutes or less until the meat starts to become a little crispy. Stir in the salt, cinnamon and pepper and fry for 1 minute, then add the boiling water.

3 Cover the pan and allow to cook over a low heat for 20 minutes. Add the spinach, lemon juice and three-quarters of the toasted pine nuts and cook for another 10 minutes. If there is still too much liquid, uncover the pan and simmer the excess liquid off for a few minutes until you have a little remaining to serve as sauce.

4 Remove from the heat and serve on a bed of Lebanese vermicelli rice (see page 239) and the lemon slices. Sprinkle the remaining pine nuts over the top.

Fish with Cumin Rice
Sayadeyeh

Sayadeyeh is a traditional fish dish. There are no rules about what fish to use as long as the flavours are maintained. Sometimes I use sea bass and sometimes whole fish or skinless fillets of chunky cod. It all depends on what's fresh or who's coming to dinner. The Lebanese always serve fish with tahini sauce.

SERVES 4

PREPARATION TIME
15 minutes

COOKING TIME
50 minutes

COOK'S TIP
You can cook the rice with a little saffron in rose water.

270g basmati rice, rinsed and left to
  soak in water
50ml olive oil
800g skinless fish, whole or fillets
2 large onions (about 300g), halved and sliced
1 tsp ground cumin
1 tsp ground cinnamon
½ tsp ground black pepper
1 tsp salt
50g almonds, toasted
20g pine nuts, toasted
A little chopped parsley, to garnish
1 vine tomato, chopped, to garnish

1 Use a little oil to shallow fry the fish in a frying pan for about 10 minutes to brown a little on each side. You can bake or steam the fish (covered in foil) if you prefer. The fish should be almost cooked through.

2 Add the remaining oil and the onions to the pan and fry for 10 minutes until the onions are soft and slightly browned. Stir in the cumin, cinnamon and black pepper and cook for 2 minutes.

3 Assemble the prepared ingredients by transferring the fried onions into a saucepan, top with the fish pieces. Drain the rice and add to the onion with salt. Add enough water to just cover the rice. Bring to the boil and allow most of the water to be absorbed by the rice. Cover, turn the heat down to low and simmer for 20 minutes and all the water is evaporated. The rice should be separated and fluffy. Remove from the heat.

4 Place a serving plate over the pan and invert. Now you have the rice in the bottom and onions on the top.

5 Scatter the almond and pine nuts over the top and garnish with chopped parsley and a little chopped tomato in the middle of the dish.

6 Serve with tahini sauce (see page 241) mixed with chopped tomatoes and chopped parsley.

Chicken with Garlic Yogurt
Fetteh Djaj

Fetteh is such a light, tasty and easy-to-make summer dish. We love *fetteh* whether it's with aubergines, chickpeas or chicken. This is a great dish to use leftover chicken with rice (*ouzy*).

SERVES 4

PREPARATION TIME
10 minutes

COOKING TIME
1 hour

COOK'S TIP
We usually assemble this dish when ready to serve, in order to prevent the bread going soggy.

1 very small whole chicken (about 800g)
150g Lebanese flatbread or pitta
1 tbsp olive oil
350g long-grain rice, soaked for 30 minutes
½ tsp salt, plus extra to season
1 tsp ground cinnamon
½ tsp ground black pepper
2 garlic cloves, crushed
600ml natural Greek yogurt
20g pine nuts, toasted
A few mint leaves, chopped
40g pomegranate seeds

1 Preheat the oven to 190ºC/Fan 170ºC/ Gas 5. Put the chicken in a roasting tin and roast for roughly 1 hour until the chicken is cooked through.

2 While the chicken is cooking, break the bread into small pieces and place them on a baking tray. Drizzle with the oil and place in the oven for 5–10 minutes until the bread is browned.

3 Drain the rice and transfer it to a saucepan. Add the salt, cinnamon and pepper. Then add hot water to just cover the surface of the rice and boil.

4 When it boils and most of the water has evaporated, cover and simmer over a low heat for roughly 15 minutes until the rice is cooked. Remove from the heat.

5 To assemble, once the chicken is cooked remove all the bones from the chicken and break the meat into small pieces.

6 Spread the rice over a serving dish, then add the chicken, followed by the toasted bread.

7 Season the crushed garlic with a little salt, then mix it with the yogurt and spread the mixture over the bread.

8 Sprinkle the pine nuts, mint and pomegranate seeds over the top and serve.

7

Salads

Opposite:
My grandsons, Dylan
and Charlie, choosing
their salad of the day.

Lebanese salads are usually simple affairs with a few ingredients and a tasty, juicy dressing.

Salads are always served to accompany a dish, mainly the drier or the more bland-flavoured ones. In these cases, the salad complements and enhances the flavours.

With our love of salads and vegetables, there is always a dish of vegetables placed on the table for eating with any meal. Children in Lebanon grow up eating lots of vegetables and always enjoy munching on raw vegetables, even for snacks.

Arabian Salad
Salata Arabeyeh

This delicious salad is served with rice dishes, such as lamb or chicken with rice, as well as many other dry vegetable dishes.

SERVES 4

PREPARATION TIME
10 minutes

COOKING TIME
none

COOK'S TIP
You may prepare this salad hours in advance and store it in the fridge. Add the dressing just before serving.

1 Put the lemon juice, garlic, salt and oil in a small jug and combine to make a salad dressing.

2 Mix all the remaining ingredients together in a bowl.

3 Just before serving, pour over the dressing to coat, then serve with rice and meat or chicken.

Juice of 1 lemon juice (about 30ml)
1–2 garlic cloves, crushed
½ tsp salt
20ml olive oil
450g tomatoes, sliced or chopped
½ large cucumber (about 180g), chopped
60g onion (1 small) or spring onions, chopped
½ red pepper (about 60g), deseeded and chopped
1 green chilli, deseeded and sliced (optional)
20g parsley, chopped
10g mint leaves, chopped

Artichoke and Tomato Salad

Salata Ardi Showki

Artichokes are frequently used in main dishes or in salads. When they're in season, you see mountains of them sold on the roadside in Lebanon, at extremely low prices.

SERVES 4

PREPARATION TIME
10 minutes

COOKING TIME
20 minutes

400g artichoke hearts, fresh or frozen
Juice of 1 lemon (about 30ml)
50g black olives
150g small vine tomatoes
10g parsley, finely chopped
2 garlic cloves, crushed
30ml olive oil
Salt

1 If using fresh artichokes, chop off the top bulk of the leaves and trim the leaves off the sides to get to the hearts.

2 Boil the artichoke hearts in water with a little salt and half the lemon juice (frozen artichoke hearts can go straight into the water without being defrosted first). Lemon juice stops the hearts from browning. Cook for 20 minutes. Check they are well cooked by pushing a fork through the centre.

3 Drain, cool and cut the hearts in halves or quarters lengthwise. Just before serving, put them in a bowl with the remaining ingredients and stir to combine.

4 Serve this salad on its own with bread or as a side.

Minty Tomato and Onion Salad

Salata Banadoura

This very simple and quick salad goes well with a wide variety of main dishes and is refreshing and tasty.

SERVES 4

PREPARATION TIME
10 minutes

COOKING TIME
none

COOK'S TIP
This is a great salad to have with *mjadra* (see page 141) and *mdardara* (see page 129).

1 Put the garlic and salt in a mortar and use the pestle to crush to a paste. Salt makes this process easier and draws out more flavour.

2 Transfer the paste to a small bowl and add the oil and lemon juice. Mix to combine.

3 Put the tomatoes, onion and mint in a salad bowl, then add the dressing. Mix and serve promptly.

1 garlic clove
½ tsp salt
1 tbsp olive oil
1 tbsp lemon juice
500g tomatoes, sliced
1 small onion (about 60g), chopped
10g mint leaves, chopped, or 1 tsp dried mint

Green Beans and Pomegranate Seeds Salad
Salata Loubeyeh Ma Rumman

I have put delicious green beans together with pomegranate seeds here. The seeds not only have a great nutritional benefit, but also add good flavour and colour.

SERVES 4

PREPARATION TIME
10 minutes

COOKING TIME
10 minutes

COOK'S TIP
Serve this salad with chicken coated with pistachios (see page 142), grilled *kafta* (see page 117) or fish with herbs and chilli (see page 170).

500g French beans, trimmed
½ tsp salt, plus extra for salting the water
Juice of 1 lemon (about 30ml)
2–3 garlic cloves, crushed
30ml olive oil
2 small gem lettuces, sliced
80g pomegranate seeds

1 Bring a pan of water to the boil. Salt the water, then add the beans and cook for 5 minutes. Remove from the heat, drain, rinse with cold water and allow the beans to dry out in a sieve.

2 Meanwhile, prepare the dressing by combining the lemon juice, garlic, oil and ½ a teaspoon of salt in a small jug.

3 Put the beans, lettuce and pomegranate seeds in a bowl, add the prepared dressing and mix all the ingredients together.

Minty Yogurt and Cucumber Salad
Salata Laban

This yogurt salad or dip is served with so many dishes, especially the ones without sauce, and it complements the flavours of any dish it's served with.

SERVES 4

PREPARATION TIME
5 minutes

COOKING TIME
none

1 Mix the crushed garlic, mint and cucumber in a bowl with the yogurt. Season with salt and stir again.

2 Garnish with the chopped fresh mint leaves and drizzle the olive oil, if using, over the top.

3 Serve as a salad on the side or as a dip.

1 garlic clove, crushed
1 tsp dried mint
½ large cucumber (about 200g), diced
500ml natural yogurt
5g fresh mint, chopped, to garnish
½ tbsp olive oil (optional)
Salt

Armenian Mixed Salad
Salata Armaniyeh

I recently had this unique and tasty, but very simple salad in Beirut at an Armenian restaurant. There is a big Armenian population in Lebanon and many Armenian dishes are integrated into Lebanese cuisine.

SERVES 4

PREPARATION TIME
10 minutes

COOKING TIME
none

1 Combine all the vegetables together in a bowl and mix gently.

2 To make the dressing, mix together the pomegranate molasses, salt, garlic and oil.

3 Add the dressing to the salad and turn gently to coat all the vegetables.

4 Serve this salad as part of the starters (maza) or as a side dish.

⅔ large cucumber (about 250g), chopped
½ red pepper (about 70g), chopped
½ green pepper (about 70g), chopped
65g spring onions, including the leaves, chopped
1 large chilli (15g), deseeded and chopped
25g pomegranate molasses
½ tsp salt, to taste
2 garlic cloves, crushed
10ml olive oil

Cabbage Salad
Salata Malfoof

This salad is an absolute favourite of mine because it can magically turn bland dishes into a delicious meal. Once you've tried it, you'll see what I mean. Cabbage provides important nutrients and is extremely high in fibre.

SERVES 4

PREPARATION TIME
10 minutes

COOKING TIME
none

COOK'S TIP
This salad goes well with *mjadra* (see page 141) and bulgur wheat with mixed vegetables (see page 109).

1 Place the shredded cabbage and pepper strips in a salad bowl.

2 For the dressing, combine the crushed garlic, salt, lemon juice and oil.

3 Add the dressing to the cabbage and mix well.

400g sweet white cabbage (flat cabbage or sweetheart variety), shredded
⅓ red pepper (about 30g), deseeded and cut into thin strips
1–2 garlic cloves, crushed
½–1 tsp salt, to taste
Juice of 1 lemon (about 30ml)
20ml olive oil

Lebanese-style Potato Salad
Salata Batata

Basic potato salad is mostly made with onions, garlic, lemon and oil.
It can be varied by adding other vegetables and herbs. Unlike most other
salads, this salad tastes better if prepared in advance.

SERVES 4

PREPARATION TIME
15 minutes

COOKING TIME
15 minutes

1kg potatoes, peeled and cut into chunks
1 tsp salt
1 small onion (about 70g), chopped
½ red pepper (about 60g), deseeded and diced
½ green pepper (about 60g), deseeded and diced
20g flat-leaf parsley, chopped
2 garlic cloves, crushed
Juice of 1 large lemon (about 40ml)
30ml olive oil

1 Boil the potatoes in plenty of water with
the salt for 15 minutes. Turn the potatoes out
into a colander, rinse with cold water and
allow to cool.

2 Once cool, cut the potatoes into smaller
cubes and place them in a bowl with the
onion, peppers and parsley.

3 Mix the crushed garlic, lemon juice
and olive oil together to make a dressing.
Add this dressing to the potato salad and
mix well.

4 Serve with kebabs, chicken or fish.

Spinach and Soya Bean Salad

Salatat Sabanekh Wsoya

My grandchildren call this salad, 'the bright green salad'. While some children may be more reluctant to eat 'green food', they like this bright tangy salad and are happy to eat it.

SERVES 4
PREPARATION TIME
5 minutes

COOKING TIME
10 minutes

300g frozen soya beans
A little salt, plus ½ tsp
1 garlic clove, crushed
Juice of 1 large lemon (about 40ml)
40ml olive oil
1 tsp mild mustard
220g baby spinach leaves
1 onion (about 80g), sliced
1 ripe avocado, sliced

1 Cook the beans in boiling water and a little salt for about 10 minutes until tender. Drain and leave to cool.

2 Prepare the dressing by mixing the garlic, ½ a teaspoon of salt, the lemon juice, oil and mustard together.

3 Put the beans and all the remaining ingredients in a bowl, pour over the dressing and mix well.

4 Serve with any meat, chicken or fish.

8

Popular Street Food

Opposite:
Sesame bread (*Caak*)
sold from a mobile
trolley.

When I am in Lebanon, I am at home. Spending four to five months there every year, I quickly get sucked into extended family life, as well as getting involved in the local community, especially being in the mountains. This is in addition to spending time with friends and being part of a great social life. And, of course, all this involves food, with food being the main focus for every occasion or get together. Therefore, a huge chunk of my time there is taken up by people's hospitality as well as returning it.

My only regret is that there is not enough time to indulge in Lebanon's street food as much as I would like.

Lebanese street food is simply the best. It is healthy, tasty and very low in cost. Outlets tend to specialise in one type of street food. For breakfast, lunch or supper you can always find a good food choice.

Falafel is always the star of the show and is enjoyed by vegans and meat lovers alike. The 'Souk el Akel' food market in the centre of Beirut is all about street food stalls. Falafel still tops the lot and there is now even a modern approach of falafel pizza for a healthier non-fried option.

The Healthy Lebanese Family Cookbook

Open Falafel Pizza
Manoushi Falafel

I first had a falafel pizza at a food market in Beirut, and now it's the latest trend in Lebanon. I really enjoyed it and liked the idea – the falafel dough is spread on the wrap and baked, then served with salad and tahini sauce on the top, which is a healthier way to eat falafel and still enjoy it just as much.

SERVES 6–8

PREPARATION TIME
20 minutes

COOKING TIME
10 minutes

COOK'S TIP
You can also serve this with added chilli sauce (see page 231)

FOR THE FALAFEL PASTE
See page 200

6–8 Lebanese wraps (if unavailable,
  use tortilla wraps)
40g tomatoes, chopped
200g little gem lettuce leaves, thinly sliced
50g flat-leaf parsley, chopped
300g pickled cucumbers, sliced or chopped
250ml tahini sauce (see page 241)

1 To make the falafel paste, follow the first 2 steps of the method on page 200, then add the baking powder.

2 Preheat the oven to 200°C/Fan 180°C/ Gas 6. Spread the falafel paste on the wrap to form a layer about 1cm thick. Then bake for 10 minutes until it looks crispy round the edges.

3 Remove the falafel pizza from the oven and top with the prepared tomatoes, lettuce, parsley and pickled cucumbers.

4 Drizzle with tahini sauce (see page 241) and serve warm.

Granddaughter Fern couldn't wait to get her hands on it!

Chickpea and Herb Patties
Falafel

Falafel is a national street food throughout the Middle East. A falafel wrap is a flatbread filled with deep-fried falafel, salad, pickles and drizzled with tahini sauce. It is usually bought from specialised falafel shops to eat on the go. Some places now serve baked falafel for a healthier option.

SERVES 6–8

PREPARATION TIME
20 minutes, plus maturing

COOKING TIME
10–15 minutes

COOK'S TIP
The falafel mixture freezes well. I always make a large batch of falafel dough and freeze it in portions. Add the baking powder when it's defrosted and you are ready to cook.

275g chickpeas, soaked overnight
275g dried split broad beans, soaked overnight, or 275g more chickpeas if broad beans are unavailable
70g coriander
60g parsley
100g spring onions, including leaves
50g garlic (1 bulb), peeled
45g ground coriander
2 tsp ground cumin
1 tsp ground black pepper
1 tsp salt
2 tsp baking powder
Sunflower oil, for frying

1 Drain the soaked chickpeas and the broad beans, if using. Then blitz them in a blender or food processor until they resemble fine breadcrumbs. Transfer them to a large mixing bowl.

2 Put the coriander, parsley, spring onions and garlic in a blender. Add the mixture to the chickpea and bean mixture with the ground coriander, cumin, pepper and salt and mix everything together thoroughly. Keep in the fridge for 4–5 hours to allow the flavours to mature.

3 Only when you're ready to cook, stir the baking powder into the refrigerated mixture and roll pieces of the falafel dough into about 12–15 small balls. Press them between the palms of your hands.

4 If frying, heat the oil and deep-fry the falafel over a medium heat for about 10 minutes until brown and cooked in the middle. Repeat until all the falafel are cooked. If baking, place the falafel patties on a greased baking tray, brush the surface with a little oil and bake in a preheated oven at 200°C/Fan 180°C/Gas 6, for 10–15 minutes.

5 Falafel is always served with chopped lettuce, tomatoes, and pickled cucumber or turnips and tahini sauce (see page 241), which is a must.

Shawarma Chicken
Shawarma Djaj

In fast-food shops you see chicken *shawarma* on a large vertical skewer. This is the home-made version and it's so simple to make.

SERVES 4–6

PREPARATION TIME
10 minutes

COOKING TIME
20 minutes

COOK'S TIP
For a quick alternative to garlic sauce, mix 2 crushed garlic cloves with 3 tablespoons of mayonnaise, a pinch of salt and a squeeze of lemon juice.

FOR THE WRAP
6 Lebanese pitta breads or any other flatbreads
200g tomatoes, chopped or sliced
150g cos or romaine lettuce leaves, thinly sliced
3–4 pickled cucumbers, sliced
2 tbsp garlic sauce (see page 238)

1 Mix the chicken and all the remaining *shawarma* ingredients together, cover and leave the chicken to marinate in the fridge for 2–3 hours or more.

2 Preheat the oven to 200°C/Fan 180°C/Gas 6. Place the chicken on a baking tray and bake for 20 minutes until the chicken is well cooked throughout.

3 Open the pitta to make a pocket, place the chicken in each wrap or pocket, add the tomatoes, lettuce and pickled cucumbers.

4 Spread some garlic sauce over the filling and fold the bread to make a wrap.

FOR THE SHAWARMA
500g skinless chicken breasts, sliced into
  small pieces
Juice of 1 lemon (about 30ml)
30ml olive oil
1 tsp ground cumin
3 garlic cloves, crushed
1 tsp salt
½ tsp ground black pepper
1 tsp paprika
1 tsp Lebanese mixed spices (see page 237)
1 tsp ground coriander
20g coriander leaves, finely chopped

Kafta Kebab Wraps
Sandwich Kebabe

Kafta is the most popular way to eat minced meat. It is served in main dishes, barbecued or in a wrap as fast food or at home.

SERVES 4

PREPARATION TIME
15 minutes

COOKING TIME
15–20 minutes

COOK'S TIP
This dish can be served just as it is instead of in a wrap, if you prefer.

8 sausage-shaped kafta (see page 203)
1 onion (about 100g), thinly sliced (optional)
10g flat-leaf parsley, chopped
25g sumac
Chilli sauce (see page 231), to taste
4 round Lebanese pitta breads or any other flatbreads
200g tomatoes, diced
Salt

1 Grill or barbecue the kafta on a high heat for 10 minutes, turning regularly, to brown on the outside.

2 Mix the onion, if using, parsley and sumac together with a little salt.

3 Spread the chilli sauce on the flatbread and place under a hot grill for 3–5 minutes until the edges brown a little.

4 Place 2 kafta kebabs on each flatbread then add equal amounts of the onion, parsley and sumac mixture and the tomatoes and roll the bread to make a wrap.

5 Serve with plain hummus (see page 39).

Spinach Triangle Pies
Fatayer Sabanekh

Spinach triangles are always served at any occasion. They can be bite-sized, medium or large. Some people prefer to make them at home but more often they are bought from bakeries to eat on the go as fast food.

MAKES ABOUT 15

PREPARATION TIME
1 hour, plus rising

COOKING TIME
15 minutes

COOK'S TIP
Spinach triangles are ideal for freezing. Freeze them separately uncooked, then once frozen put them in a freezer-proof bag together. Bake straight from frozen, as above, adding 5 minutes to the cooking time.

FOR THE DOUGH
400g plain flour, wholemeal or mixed, plus extra for rolling
2 tsp instant dried yeast
½ tsp salt
About 230ml warm water
2 tbsp oil, plus extra for brushing

FOR THE FILLING
200g spinach, chopped
30ml olive oil
1 onion (about 150g), chopped
Juice of 1 lemon (about 30ml)
2 tsp sumac
1 tsp salt

1 Prepare the dough by mixing the flour, yeast and salt together. Gradually add warm water while kneading until you have a smooth dough that doesn't stick to your hands and has no clumps of flour. Cover and leave the dough somewhere warm for about 2 hours to rise until doubled in size.

2 Meanwhile, mix together all the filling ingredients, then set aside until you roll the dough.

3 Preheat the oven to 220°C/Fan 200°C/ Gas 7.

4 When the dough is ready, knock it back, then roll it out very thinly on a floured surface. Cut out circles of about 10cm in diameter. Place a dessertspoon of the filling on each circle. Seal each circle by lifting up 2 sides and pressing them firmly together, then seal the third side to make a triangle shape (see photographs).

5 Place the triangles on a greased baking tray, brush the surface with a little oil and bake for 15 minutes until golden brown. Serve warm or cold.

Lamb Pizza
Lahem Bajeen

This traditional Lebanese pizza (*manoushi*), is classed as street food. It is a speciality of Baalbek (city of the sun), which was a Roman settlement in the Beka'a Valley. When visiting the Roman ruins and temples, you head for a *lahem bajeen* before you leave.

MAKES 4

PREPARATION TIME
20 minutes, plus rising

COOKING TIME
10 minutes

COOK'S TIP
Small *lahem bajeen* are popular for parties as canapés.

2 tsp instant dried yeast
½ tsp salt
300g bread flour, plus extra for rolling
30ml olive oil
200ml warm water

FOR THE TOPPING
1 small onion (about 50g)
½ red pepper (about 70g)
70g tomato
200g minced lamb
1 tsp salt
½ tsp ground black pepper
20g pomegranate seeds (optional)

1 Mix the yeast and salt with the flour, rub in the oil and gradually add the water, then knead to form a soft, smooth dough. Cover the bowl and place it in a warm place for up to 2 hours, until the dough doubles in size.

2 Put the onion, red pepper and tomato in a food processor, and blitz, then combine with the minced lamb, salt and pepper.

3 Preheat the oven to 220ºC/Fan 200ºC/ Gas 7. When the dough has risen, knock it back and divide it into 4 equal pieces. Roll each piece out thinly to a diameter of 20cm on a floured surface.

4 Before you're ready to put the pizzas in the oven, spread the topping over the surface of each dough circle. Bake in the oven for 10 minutes until the edges are a little brown and crispy.

5 Remove from the oven, sprinkle with pomegranate seeds, if using, and serve with your choice of lemon wedges, chilli sauce (see page 23) or plain yogurt for dipping.

Cheese or Zaatar Pizza
Manoushi

Manoushis are a breakfast street food. The specialist bakeries that sell them, which are found in every street, open only until midday. Manoushis are made with different toppings – halloumi cheese or zaatar (wild thyme) mixed with olive oil or lamb (to make lahem bajeen). They are also made at home at weekends when the family gets together for breakfast.

MAKES 8–10

PREPARATION TIME
20 minutes

COOKING TIME
40 minutes

COOK'S TIP
Manoushis are often made small for buffets and as canapés. Zaatar is usually bought already mixed with sumac and sesame seeds. If yours is already mixed, you won't need the sumac and sesame seeds listed above.

FOR THE DOUGH
500g plain flour, plus extra for rolling
7g instant dried yeast
1 tsp salt
300ml warm water

FOR THE TOPPINGS
10g zaatar (but see Cook's Tip)
10g sesame seeds, toasted (but see Cook's Tip)
5g sumac (but see Cook's Tip)
½ tsp salt
60ml olive oil
500g low-salt halloumi cheese, grated

1 Make the dough following the same method as for the Lebanese flatbread (see page 234).

2 Mix together the zaatar, toasted sesame seeds, sumac and salt (but see Cook's Tip). Add the oil and mix well until you have a slightly runny paste.

3 When the dough is ready, tip it out onto a floured surface and divide it into 8–10 balls.

4 Preheat the oven to 240°C/Fan 220°C/ Gas 9. Roll out the balls into circles of about ½cm thick. Spread the zaatar topping over half the rolled dough and spread the halloumi cheese over the other half.

5 Place the manoushi on a heated baking tray and tap the surface of the dough with your fingers to make dents so that the dough doesn't rise and fill with hot air.

6 Bake the manoushi for 10 minutes in a preheated oven until they brown a little around the edges. Serve warm.

9

Natural Sweet Treats

Opposite:
Granddaughters
Florence and Amba
sharing a dessert with
spoons and fingers.

In Lebanon, fresh fruits are the most popular choice to have after a meal. Hosts will always offer a selection of fruit to guests. Dried fruits, which you might have with tea or coffee, or on the rare occasion there's no fresh fruit, are always available and are mainly dried figs and dates. Sweet treats, on the other hand, might be eaten with coffee, but never directly after a meal.

We have a huge variety of Middle Eastern cakes (*baklawa*), pancakes filled with walnuts and a number of others that are soaked in syrup. Dates are commonly used in cakes and other treats. Here, I have selected only a few old-fashioned sweet dishes that don't require any added sugar. They are naturally sweetened with dried fruit and sometimes with molasses.

Apricots with Yogurt and Pistachio Pots

Laban Ma'a Meshmoush

Recently, while staying with my daughter, I made this dish for dessert. My granddaughters, Florence and Amba, absolutely loved it and now ask for it freqently.

SERVES 4–5

PREPARATION TIME
5 minutes

COOKING TIME
15 minutes

1 Put the apricots and the orange juice in a small pan over a medium heat. Bring to a simmer then reduce the heat to low, cover and cook for 15 minutes until the mixture looks thick and syrupy. Remove from the heat.

2 Allow the apricot and juice mixture to cool, then add the flower water, if using.

3 Using either 1 large serving bowl or 4 or 5 individual dessert dishes layer the yogurt alternately with the apricot mixture and top with the crushed pistachios.

5 Refrigerate for 30 minutes before serving cold.

300g soft dried apricots, roughly chopped
300ml pure orange juice
½ tbsp orange blossom water (mazaher)
  (optional)
400g natural Greek yogurt
50g pistachios, crushed

Semolina and Date Cookies
Maamool

These cookies are traditionally made at Easter time, but can be bought at patisseries all year round. They are filled with dates, crushed pistachios or walnuts.

MAKES **24**

PREPARATION TIME
1 hour, plus resting

COOKING TIME
30 minutes, plus
resting time

COOK'S TIP
Maamools keep for
several weeks if kept
in an airtight
container and they
are also suitable for
freezing.

250g semolina
150g plain flour
1 tsp instant dried yeast
2 tsp baking powder
2 tsp ground mahlab (if available –
   can be bought online)
200g unsalted butter, melted
1 tbsp orange blossom water (mazaher)
2 tbsp rose water (maward)
100ml milk

FOR THE FILLING
350g dates, stoned and puréed
70g walnuts, chopped
50g salted butter, melted

1 Mix the semolina, flour, yeast, baking powder and mahlab together. Then pour the melted butter into the flour mixture. Add the flower waters and milk and mix to form a smooth dough. Cover the dough and leave it to rest for at least 6 hours before using.

2 Make the filling by combining the puréed dates, chopped walnuts and melted butter together in a bowl.

3 Preheat the oven to 190ºC/Fan 170ºC/ Gas 5. Knead the dough a little to soften it, then divide it into 24 small balls, each about the size of a golf ball. Flatten each one in the palm of your hands. Take a piece of the date filling, about 20g, flatten it, place it in the centre of the dough and wrap it with the dough.

4 As the moulds for the maamool pattern are not easily available, just make any pattern on the surface of the dough with a fork.

5 Place the maamools on a sheet of baking parchment on a baking tray, leaving space in between each one so they have space to expand.

6 Bake in the oven for 30–35 minutes until they are lightly browned.

Date and Tahini Truffles
Tamer Ma Tahini

Dates are such an important fruit in all Middle Eastern countries. They are always served with coffee and in cakes. During the month of Ramadan, after fasting from sunrise until sunset, people break the fast with dates before starting the meal. Since ancient times, it has been known that, eaten in moderation, dates provide instant energy and revitalise the body. They are easily digested, and contain fibre and iron and other minerals.

MAKES 25–30

PREPARATION TIME
40 minutes

COOKING TIME
none

COOK'S TIP
Date truffles will keep
for several weeks in
an airtight container.

120g almonds
350g dates, pitted
70g tahini

FOR THE COATINGS
20g unsweetened desiccated coconut
30g pistachios, chopped
30g almonds, chopped

1 Chop the almonds in a food processor until they resemble breadcrumbs.

2 Chop the dates using a food processor, then mix the chopped dates with the tahini and 4 tablespoons of water and blend together until they form a paste. Combine with the almonds.

3 Roll the date mixture between the palms of your hands to make 25–30 small balls of 3–4cm in diameter.

4 Roll each date ball in one of the coating ingredients.

5 Place the truffle-like date balls in the fridge for 1 hour before serving, with tea or coffee.

Semolina and Walnut Cake

Ka'ket Maamool

Traditionally, you'd find this served as small individual cakes served with coffee. However, after the first time I had *maamool* cake in a Beirut restaurant, I liked the idea of serving it as a dessert.

SERVES 4–6

PREPARATION TIME
20 minutes, plus resting

COOKING TIME
30 minutes

COOK'S TIP
This is delicious served with ice cream.

100g semolina
50g plain flour
1 tsp instant dried yeast
1 tsp baking powder
100g unsalted butter, melted
1 tbsp orange blossom water (mazaher)
2 tbsp rose water (maward)
30ml milk

FOR THE FILLING
200g walnuts, chopped
1 tbsp orange flower water (mazaher)
1 tbsp rose water (maward)
2 tbsp honey or date molasses
Icing sugar, for dusting

1 Mix the semolina, flour, yeast and baking powder together. Pour in the melted butter, then add the flower waters and milk and mix to form a smooth dough. Cover the dough and allow it to rest for at least 5–6 hours before using.

2 Mix the walnuts, flower waters and honey or date molasses together to form a paste.

3 Preheat the oven to 190°C/Fan 170°C/ Gas 5. Roll out the *maamool* pastry to about 30cm. Place the filling in the middle and fold over the pastry to cover.

4 Place the cake on a piece of baking parchment on a baking tray and score the surface with a knife into serving portions.

5 Bake for 30 minutes until the surface is slightly brown.

6 Take the cake out of the oven and while it is still hot, dust it with icing sugar. The dish can be served warm or cold.

Lebanese Fruit Salad with Honey and Curd
Salata Fwakeh Wkashta

Lebanese fruit salad is not just a fruit salad. It's deliciously rich with the combination of all the different flavours. You may use any fresh, seasonal fruit. Here, I used fruit that can be found in Lebanon during autumn.

SERVES 6

PREPARATION TIME
20 minutes

COOKING TIME
none

1 large pear (about 200g)
1 large banana
200g green grapes
200g persimmon fruit
200g purple plums
200g black grapes
60g pomegranate seeds
50g pistachio nuts
30g pine nuts
20ml orange blossom water (mazaher)

FOR THE TOPPING
6 tbsp milk curd (see page 243)
3 tbsp honey, for drizzling
20g pistachios, chopped

1 Chop all the fruit into bite-sized pieces, cutting all the grapes in half.

2 Place the prepared fruit in a bowl with the pomegranate seeds. Add the pistachios, pine nuts and orange blossom water and mix gently.

3 Serve each portion in a glass bowl. Top with 1 tablespoon of curd, drizzle with ½ a tablespoon of honey and sprinkle with a few ground pistachios.

4 Serve chilled. (This is seriously delicious!)

No Sugar and No Egg Cake
Sfoof be Debes

Sfoof is a very old-fashioned cake and this version comes primarily from the mountains, where it's especially popular during Lent. It's most commonly made with turmeric, which turns it yellow. I doubt there's a simpler cake to bake.

SERVES 6–8

PREPARATION TIME
5–10 minutes

COOKING TIME
35–40 minutes

½ tbsp aniseeds
130g semolina
130g plain flour
2 tsp ground aniseed
2 tsp baking powder
200ml olive oil
200ml carob molasses
½ tbsp tahini, for greasing
20g sesame seeds

1 Put 1 cup of water into a small saucepan and bring to the boil. Add the aniseeds and simmer for 5 minutes until the volume is reduced by three-quarters. Drain, reserving the water.

2 Preheat the oven to 180ºC/Fan 160ºC/ Gas 4. Mix the semolina, flour, ground aniseed and baking powder together in a mixing bowl.

3 Add the oil, molasses and aniseed cooking water and whisk all the ingredients together for 1 minute until it looks smooth.

4 Grease a 20cm round or square loose-bottomed cake tin with the tahini, and pour in the mixture. Sprinkle the sesame seeds evenly over the top.

5 Bake the cake in the oven for 35–40 minutes.

Dried Apricot and Nuts Dessert
Mhallabeyeht El Mishmoush

I wasn't planning to include desserts in this book, but then I thought why not include delicious, sugarless treats that are packed with goodness. This dessert is made with nutritious, healthy ingredients and a natural sweetness comes from the apricots. The orange blossom water (*mazaher*) adds both flavour and aroma.

SERVES 4

PREPARATION TIME
10 minutes, plus
soaking

COOKING TIME
10 minutes

200g dried ready-to-eat apricots
300ml warm water
300g pistachios
20g pine nuts
35g split almonds
35g cashews
15g cornflour
½ tbsp orange blossom water (mazaher)

1 Put the apricots in a bowl and pour over the warm water. Leave to soak overnight.

2 Soak all the nuts in cold water for about 2 hours.

3 Purée the apricots with any excess water in a food processor until the apricots are smooth and creamy. Turn the purée out into a small saucepan.

4 Mix the cornflour in 50ml of cold water until any lumps have disappeared, then pour it into the pan with the apricot purée.

5 Place the saucepan over a medium heat. Stir continuously for about 7 minutes and when the purée begins to boil, turn down the heat to low and continue to cook for 3 minutes until it thickens.

6 Divide the purée into 4 individual bowls and allow to cool.

7 Drain the nuts and dry with kitchen paper, then sprinkle them over the portions of apricot purée. Chill in the fridge for 1–2 hours before serving.

Semolina Fig Slices
Ka'ak Teen

Figs are high in natural sugars, minerals and soluble fibre and are a good source of antioxidants. They are excellent for a healthy digestive system if eaten fresh or dried. Dried figs are also excellent for jam.

SERVES 6–8

PREPARATION TIME
10 minutes, plus resting

COOKING TIME
30–35 minutes

160g coarse semolina
160g fine semolina or plain flour
1 tsp dried instant yeast
2 tsp baking powder
100g unsalted butter, melted
50ml milk
1 tbsp rose water (maward)
100g icing sugar (optional)

FOR THE FILLING
400g soft dried figs
½ apple (about 55g), cored
½ orange (about 65g), with rind
1 tsp ground cinnamon
65g walnuts, roughly chopped

1 Mix the semolina, fine semolina or flour, yeast and baking powder together thoroughly. Pour in the melted butter to absorb the dry ingredients. Add the milk and rose water and mix to form a smooth dough. Cover the dough and allow it to rest for at least 5–6 hours before using.

2 Blitz the figs, apple, orange and cinnamon with 30ml of water in a food processor to make a thick paste. Add the walnuts and mix well.

3 Preheat the oven to 190°C/Fan 170°C/Gas 5. Roll out the semolina dough into a long strip about 1cm thick. Place the fig mixture in the middle and fold the dough from the long sides over the figs and seal.

4 Place the filled dough on a piece of baking parchment on a baking tray and score the surface with a knife.

5 Bake in the oven for 30–35 minutes until you have a slightly browned dough.

6 If icing the fig slices, cream the icing sugar with a little water.

7 Remove the tray from the oven and cool the fig roll. Cut through the scoring lines. Transfer the slices to a serving plate and drizzle with a little icing.

Date Slices with Nuts
Tamreyeh

People buy date slices, but I've never been tempted to buy them as they are so easily made at home. They can be made in no time and, of course, they are more delicious than the shop-bought ones.

MAKES ABOUT
20 SLICES

PREPARATION TIME
15 minutes, plus
refrigeration

COOKING TIME
none

1 Blitz the dates in a food processor together with the butter to form a paste, or just mix by hand.

2 Mix the minced dates with the biscuits and walnuts.

3 On a smooth surface, roll the date mixture into a sausage shape, then roll it in the desiccated coconut to coat it all over.

4 Wrap the coconut-covered date mixture in cling film and refrigerate for 2 hours until firm.

5 Remove the cling film and slice the sausage shape into 1–2cm-thick slices.

6 Keep the date slices in the fridge in a sealed container (the slices will stick together at room temperature). These are a real treat with coffee.

500g block of pitted dates
60g unsalted butter, melted
80g rich tea biscuits, broken into small pieces
100g walnuts, crushed
40g unsweetened desiccated coconut

10

Basic Reference Recipes

Opposite:
Lebanese bread (*khibs*)
is baked in a small local
bakery.

A leaf of Sa'aj bread. Mona Hamadeh at Ibtesam's village bakery with Ibtesam.

This chapter contains recipes I use repeatedly throughout the book. I always like to keep them separate from other recipes, so you can refer to them easily.

These recipes are easily made with very few ingredients, which makes them simpler to remember and quicker to get to know, so you'll soon find you won't have to look them up each time.

Rice is a common accompaniment to meals, but we sometimes flavour it according to the dish it is being served with. Vermicelli rice is the most traditional and most popular. Plain rice is preferred when served with strong-flavoured food. Saffron rice is both colourful and aromatic and complements fish and chicken dishes. I highly recommend cumin rice with fish.

Bulgur wheat is sometimes used to substitute rice or served with salad.

It is worth culturing your own yogurt, which is simple to make, better tasting and much cheaper than buying. Making labneh (concentrated yogurt) is the most popular kind of cream cheese, always served at breakfast, as a dip with olives, garlic and onions. A labneh wrap is a wonderful, quick snack with salad, herbs and olives.

Making Lebanese pitta bread is fun and simple, and the result is delicious. There are several varieties of bread making. The most common are a flat pitta-type bread and a Sa'aj bread, which is a very thin leaf of dough cooked individually on a large dome, heated by the fire under it.

Chilli Sauce
Salsa Harrah

This sauce is so simple and quick to make that you will say goodbye to any chilli sauce that comes in a jar. You can modify it if you prefer it milder or hotter, simply by using fewer or more chillis.

MAKES ABOUT 300G

PREPARATION TIME
10 minutes

COOKING TIME
15 minutes

2 long red peppers (about 250g)
3 red chillies
Juice of ¼ lemon (about 10ml)
½ tbsp olive oil
Salt

1 Preheat the oven to 200ºC/Fan 180ºC/Gas 6. Put the peppers and chillies in a roasting tin and place in the oven for 15 minutes.

2 Remove the peppers and chillies from the oven and cover them with foil while cooling. This makes it easier to peel off the skin.

3 After peeling the skin and removing the seeds, chop everything in a food processor until it forms a paste. Add the lemon juice, olive oil and salt and combine.

4 Serve with any grilled meat or fish, or spread on flatbread to make a simple chilli bread. Keep the sauce in a jar in the fridge. It will keep for up to 10 days.

Chilli Bread
Khibez Harr

Chilli bread complements barbecued meat and kafta kebabs brilliantly. It makes a meaty wrap very special with all the different flavours in the bread alone.

1 Lebanese flatbread or other flatbread
1 tbsp chilli sauce (see page 231)
2 vine tomatoes (about 200g),
    deseeded and diced
5g parsley, chopped
Salt

1 Lightly grill the bread on one side for 1–2 minutes. Remove the bread from the grill, spread the chilli sauce all over the uncooked side of the bread and top with the chopped tomatoes.

2 Return the bread to the grill, tomato side up, and cook for 2 more minutes until the edge of the bread is brown and crispy.

3 Remove from the grill, season with a sprinkle of salt over the tomatoes and top with the chopped parsley.

4 Serve with barbecued meat, as an individual wrap, or with dips and salads.

Saffron Rice
Rouz Bzafaran

I like saffron rice with certain dishes – mainly with fish and chicken, which are complemented by the aroma and flavour. I keep a few threads of saffron in rose water or plain water in a jar for when needed.
By soaking the saffron you will get more flavour and a brighter yellow colour. Rose water provides an additional aromatic flavour that complements the saffron.

SERVES 4

PREPARATION TIME
5 minutes, plus soaking

COOKING TIME
15 minutes

COOK'S TIP
Sometimes I garnish the top of the rice with a small, thinly sliced onion fried until crispy and brown. This looks pretty and adds flavour.

400g basmati rice
½ tsp salt
Pinch of saffron threads, pre-soaked
  in a little water

1 Rinse the rice well to rinse away the starch, which can cause the rice to stick. Then leave to soak in warm water for 30 minutes to 1 hour.

2 Put the rice in a saucepan, add the salt and pour in water to about 1cm above the rice level (too much water will make the rice sticky and stodgy). Place over a medium heat and cook for 15 minutes until the water has been absorbed. Then drain the rice.

3 Add the saffron and its soaking water to the rice, give the rice a quick stir with a fork, cover and simmer over a low heat for 10 more minutes until the rice is dry and fluffy.

Lebanese Flatbread
Khibez

Bread is our basic source of carbohydrate and is present at every meal. Some people even take every mouthful of food with a piece of bread. This flatbread is great for wraps and has a hollow pocket you can fill with any food your like!

MAKES 8 PITTAS

PREPARATION TIME
15 minutes, plus
rising and resting

COOKING TIME
7–10 minutes

COOK'S TIP
I make a large batch
of bread, bake them,
allow them to cool,
then push out the air
so that the breads are
flat and I can freeze
them for another
time.

330g wholemeal bread flour or white if preferred, plus extra for rolling
2 tsp instant dried yeast
½ tsp salt
About 200ml warm water

1 In a large bowl, thoroughly, mix together all the dry ingredients. Gradually add the water while mixing all the time. Knead the dough for a few minutes, so it's smooth and has no flour pockets.

2 Cover the bowl with cling film and leave it in a warm place, with a minimum temperature of 22°C/72°F for 2 hours or until the dough has doubled in size.

3 Preheat the oven to 240°C/Fan 220°C/Gas 9. Put two baking trays into the oven to heat as the oven warms up. (Pizza oven stones are perfect for making breads as well as pizzas.) Knead the dough again on a floured surface to knock it back and divide it into 8 equally sized balls.

4 Roll each dough ball into smooth round circles about ½ cm thick. Leave all 8 circles on a floured surface for 10 minutes to rest. It is important to make sure there are no dents on the surfaces of the rolled circles, because this will prevent the loaf from splitting and forming a good pocket.

5 Place the rolled dough on the heated baking trays and bake in the oven for 7–10 minutes. Each flatbread will puff out and become slightly brown. You may need to bake the bread in batches. Serve with dips, or at any meal for scooping food.

Cultured Yogurt
Laban

A Lebanese household is never without a large pot of yogurt in the fridge. This is because yogurt is consumed regularly, mostly for dressing, salads and making *labneh* cheese.

MAKES **2** LITRES

PREPARATION TIME
5 minutes, plus
cooling and setting

COOKING TIME
20 minutes

COOK'S TIP
Reserve a little yogurt
from your own culture
to use for the next
batch.

2 litres full-fat or semi-skimmed milk
150g natural yogurt

1 Boil the milk over a medium to low heat for 20 minutes, giving it a stir every few minutes to prevent it from sticking to the bottom of the pan.

2 When the milk boils and begins to rise to the top of the pan, take it off the heat.

3 Allow the milk to cool and reach body temperature. I still use the old-fashioned method of dipping my (very clean) little finger in the milk and counting up to 10. You should just start feeling the heat when you get to 10.

4 Put the yogurt in a bowl and cream with a spoon, so there are no lumps. Stir in the milk until fully combined.

5 Cover the bowl and place it in a warm place, such as an airing cupboard, or in a room with a normal room temperature, covered over with a towel or a small blanket for extra warmth.

6 Leave the milk undisturbed for at least 6 hours to set. Any slight movement of the milk will disturb the culture and stop it from setting and turning into yogurt. Once set, the yogurt can be kept in a covered bowl or dish in the fridge. It will keep for up to 10 days.

Mixed Seven Spice
Sabaa Bharat

Seven spice is found in Middle Eastern shops, some western supermarkets, and online. Alternatively, it is worth investing in a little grinder to grind your own spices. Once you start you'll never go back to buying packets.

MAKES ABOUT 150G

PREPARATION TIME
5 minutes

COOKING TIME
none

40g cinnamon sticks
15g dried ginger
15g nutmeg
40g allspice
20g black peppercorns
10g cardamom pods
15g coriander seeds

1 Put all your spices in the grinder and grind for 1 minute.

2 When the spices have turned into a brown powder, transfer them to an airtight jar. This will keep for months.

Traditional Garlic Sauce
Salsat Toom

Garlic sauce is always used as a condiment for roasted or barbecued chicken. You can also use it as a marinade for chicken, and drizzled over salad. This is such a useful recipe, if you love garlic, of course.

MAKES ABOUT 1 CUP
(250ML)

PREPARATION TIME
10 minutes

COOKING TIME
none

COOK'S TIP
This sauce will taste better the next day when the garlic will be less powerful. It will keep in the fridge for up to 2 weeks.

60g garlic cloves
200ml corn or nut oil
Juice of 1–2 lemons (about 20ml)
¼ tsp salt

1 Peel the garlic cloves and process them in a food processor until puréed.

2 With the motor still running, gradually drizzle in the oil until you've used it all up.

3 Add the lemon juice and salt to the garlic and oil mixture and combine thoroughly.

You should have a fluffy white sauce, like whipped cream.

4 Turn the sauce out into a container, cover and keep it in the fridge until the following day.

5 Serve as a condiment with chicken or other meat, or as a starter spread on sliced tomatoes sprinkled with sumac and drizzled with olive oil. This is often served with the maza selection as a low-calorie dish, plus it's simple and tasty.

Lebanese Vermicelli Rice

Rouz be Shayriyeh

This is the most common and delicious way to eat rice. Most Lebanese people will cook rice only in this way. When I was a child and my mother was too busy to cook, we had to make do with vermicelli rice and natural yogurt on top of it as a meal – we loved it. My children grew up on Lebanese food and were used to rice being served often. When I made food without rice for more than one day, they would accuse me of being lazy!

SERVES 4

PREPARATION TIME
2 minutes, plus soaking

COOKING TIME
20 minutes

1 Rinse the rice to wash off all the starch until the water looks clear. Soak in water and set aside for 30 minutes to 1 hour, then drain.

2 Heat the butter or oil in a saucepan, add the vermicelli and fry over a medium heat for 3 minutes until golden brown. Drain off the excess fat and add the rice and salt. Add water to cover the rice by 1cm. Bring to the boil.

3 When most of the water has been absorbed, cover the pan and simmer over a low heat for 15 minutes. Stir only once half way through cooking.

400g basmati or any long-grain rice
30g butter or olive oil
60g vermicelli, lightly crushed
½ tsp salt

Cumin Rice
Rouz Bkammoun

Cumin rice is so simple and flavoursome and complements both fish and chicken dishes.

SERVES 4

PREPARATION TIME
5 minutes

COOKING TIME
25 minutes

20ml olive oil
3 tsp cumin seeds
1 small onion (about 80–100g), chopped
400g basmati rice, soaked for 30 minutes
1 tsp salt
½ tsp ground black pepper

1 Heat the oil in a saucepan, add the cumin seeds and keep turning until they begin to pop.

2 Add the onion and fry it with the cumin for 7–10 minutes until softened and slightly brown.

3 Drain the rice and add it to the onion with the salt and pepper. Add water to cover the surface of the rice by 1cm. Bring to the boil.

4 When most of the water has been absorbed, cover the pan and simmer over a low heat for 15 minutes, turning the rice once while cooking.

Tahini Sauce
Tarator

In Lebanon we use tahini so frequently that we usually buy it by the litre!
It is used in dishes and dips, but is mostly used as a sauce.

MAKES 200ML

PREPARATION TIME
5 minutes

COOKING TIME
none

100g tahini
Juice of 1 lemon (about 30ml)
1 garlic clove, crushed
½ tsp salt

1 Put the tahini in a bowl and add the lemon juice. Mix until it turns thick and fluffy.

2 Gradually add a little water at a time and keep mixing, making sure there are no lumps before you add more water. Keep adding a little water until you have a smooth creamy texture.

3 Add the garlic and salt and stir to combine.

4 This tahini sauce is always served with fish and with some roasted vegetables. Sometimes it is used in dips or as salad dressing.

Bulgur Wheat with Tomatoes
Burghul ma Banadoura or Plain

Bulgur wheat (burghul) is so frequently used in Lebanese cooking. We use it in our national dishes, in peasant food, and as a substitute for rice, which most rural people prefer. When wheat is harvested in the summer, people make their own burghul to store for the whole year.

SERVES 4

PREPARATION TIME
5 minutes

COOKING TIME
30 minutes

COOK'S TIP
To make a version without tomatoes, cook the onions, then add the bulgur wheat and water. Cover the pan and simmer for 20 minutes until all the water has evaporated.

1 large onion (about 200g), chopped
40ml olive oil
380g tomatoes, chopped (optional)
250g coarse bulgur wheat (burghul),
  rinsed and drained
1 tsp salt
½ tsp ground black pepper

1 Put the onion and oil in a saucepan and fry over a medium heat for 10 minutes until the onion is almost brown.

2 Add the tomatoes, if using, and the salt and pepper, cover the pan and simmer for 2–3 minutes to get the juice out of the tomatoes.

3 Add the bulgur wheat and stir. If the tomatoes are dry, add water to just the same level as the bulgur wheat, then simmer for 10–15 minutes, until all the liquid has been absorbed.

4 Serve with any stew, fish or chicken, or just with salad.

Milk Curd

Kashta

Kashta has been known in the Arab world for centuries. It is the thickest part of the whey, used as cake filler and in desserts and is mostly served as 'curd and honey', which is extremely hard to resist.

SERVES 4

PREPARATION TIME
2 minutes

COOKING TIME
15–20 minutes

COOK'S TIP
To serve the *kashta* (curd) with a dessert, mix it with 200ml whipped cream before making, otherwise it can be a little dry.

1 litre full-fat milk
Juice of 1 lemon (about 30ml)

1 Boil the milk over a medium heat, stirring it occasionally so it doesn't stick to the bottom of the pan. As soon as it begins to rise to the top of the pan, add the lemon juice. After 1 or 2 minutes, the milk will begin to separate from the whey and form cheese-like lumps – curd. Scoop the curd up with a slotted spoon and put it in a sieve until all the whey has been drained out.

2 Serve with fruit salad or as the traditional curd and honey (see page 25).

Index

Freekeh with Peppers and Tomatoes 82
Freekeh Salad 89
fruit salad 221

G
garlic 13
  garlic sauce 238
green beans
  Bulgur Wheat with Mixed Vegetables 109
  Green Beans and Pomegranate Seeds Salad
    188
  Green and White Beans with Tomato and
    Garlic 175
  Mediterranean Vegetables and Lamb Bake 157

H
hummus
  Hummus with Kafta Balls 39
  Hummus with Parsley and Pine Nuts 48

I
ingredients, main 11–14

K
Kafta with Aubergine Bake 105
Kafta, Grilled, and Peppers 117
Kafta Kebab Wraps 203
Kafta Meatballs in Tomato Sauce 145
Kafta Toasties 78
kashta 243

L
labneh 20
lamb
  Aleppo-style Kebab 162
  Aubergines Filled with Minced Meat 110
  Bean Stew 173
  Eggs with Lamb 19
  Grilled Kafta and Peppers 117
  Hummus with Kafta Balls 39
  Kafta with Aubergine Bake 105
  Kafta Kebab Wraps 203
  Kafta Meatballs in Tomato Sauce 145

Kafta Toasties 78
  Lamb and Aubergine Casserole 146
  Lamb Pizza 206
  Mediterranean Vegetables and Lamb Bake 157
  Okra with Lamb 122
Lebanese Flatbread 234
Lebanese Fruit Salad with Honey and Curd 221
lemons 12
lentils
  Lentil and Rainbow Chard Soup 91
  Lentils and Bulgur Wheat 165
  Lentils with Spinach 158
  Lentils with Wholegrain Rice and
    Caramelised Onions 129
  Red Lentil Soup 81
  Red Split Lentils with Bulgur Wheat 47
light meals and sides 56–97

M
main dishes 98–181
manoushi see pizza
maza 26–55
milk curd 243
  Lebanese Fruit Salad with Honey and Curd 221
mint 13

N
nuts
  Aleppo-style Kebab 162
  Apricots with Yogurt and Pistachio Pots 213
  Chicken Coated with Pistachios 142
  Chicken with Rice and Nuts 126
  Date Slices with Nuts 227
  Date and Tahini Truffles 217
  Dried Apricots and Nuts Dessert 225
  Semolina and Date Cookies 214
  Semolina Fig Slices 226
  Semolina and Walnut Cake 218

O
Okra with Lamb 122
olive oil 11
olives 11